OXFORD SLAVONIC PAPERS

Edited by

ROBERT AUTY J. L. I. FENNELL

and

I. P. FOOTE

General Editor

NEW SERIES

VOLUME VII

OXFORD

AT THE CLARENDON PRESS

1974

Oxford University Press, Ely House, London W. 1

GLASGOW NEW YORK TORONTO MELBOURNE WELLINGTON
CAPE TOWN IBADAN NAIROBI DAR ES SALAAM LUSAKA ADDIS ABABA
DELHI BOMBAY CALCUTTA MADRAS KARACHI LAHORE DACCA
KUALA LUMPUR SINGAPORE HONG KONG TOKYO

ISBN 8156472

Printed in Great Britain
at the University Press, Oxford
by Vivian Ridler
Printer to the University

THE editorial policy of the New Series of *Oxford Slavonic Papers* in general follows that of the original series, thirteen volumes of which appeared between the years 1950 and 1967 under the editorship of Professor S. Konovalov (volumes 11 to 13 edited jointly with Mr. J. S. G. Simmons, who also acted as General Editor of the New Series, volumes 1 to 4). It is devoted to the publication of original contributions and documents relating to the languages, literatures, culture, and history of Russia and the other Slavonic countries, and appears annually towards the end of the year. Reviews of individual books will not normally be included, but bibliographical and review articles are envisaged.

The British System of Cyrillic transliteration (British Standard 2979: 1958) has been adopted, omitting diacritics and using -y to express -й, -ий, -ій, and -ый at the end of proper names, e.g. Sergey, Dostoevsky, Bely, Grozny. For philological work the International System (ISO R/9) is used.

ROBERT AUTY
J. L. I. FENNELL
I. P. FOOTE

The Queen's College, Oxford

CONTENTS

B. O. Unbegaun's Contributions to Russian and Slavonic Philology

By ROBERT AUTY

I

THE death of Boris Ottokar Unbegaun on 4 March 1973 deprived Russian and Slavonic linguistic studies of one of their foremost representatives. His loss is keenly felt by his colleagues the world over, and particularly in the three countries where he successively held professorial chairs, France, England, and the United States. He contributed several articles to the First Series of *Oxford Slavonic Papers*, and it seems appropriate to attempt here an appreciation of his contributions to scholarship.[1]

When surveying the long series of articles and books which he published between the appearance of his first review in Ljubljana in 1923 and his death fifty years later we are first struck by the wide range of subjects covered and of the languages in which they are dealt with. Unbegaun wrote with precision, fluency, and wit in four languages, his native Russian, French, German, and English. Although the themes which he investigated were extremely varied they may all be seen as developing from the studies and training of his early years; and they show a unity of approach which derives on the one hand from the philological method which never allows the study of language to move far from the study of actual texts, and on the other hand from the profound conviction that language is primarily to be viewed as an expression and illustration of the life of men. Unbegaun was wont to describe his insatiable, ironical but at the same time sympathetic, curiosity about the infinite variety of human behaviour, past and present, as the study of *vergleichende Kultur- und Sittengeschichte*. Language for him was always connected above all with life.

It was at Ljubljana in the early 1920s that he was initiated into the study of Slavonic philology by those brilliant representatives of the neogrammarian tradition at its best, Rajko Nahtigal and Fran Ramovš. Then, in Paris, he sat at the feet of Antoine Meillet, who enabled him to see the Slavonic languages in a wider Indo-European perspective,

---

[1] A bibliography of Unbegaun's publications up to the end of 1967 appeared in *Annuaire de l'Institut de philologie et d'histoire orientales et slaves*, xviii (1966–7) (Brussels, 1968), ix–xxx. Several, though by no means all, of his publications after that date are referred to in the present article. Articles which were reprinted in B. O. Unbegaun, *Selected Papers on Russian and Slavonic Philology* (Oxford, 1969) are referred to by page references to that volume which hereinafter appears abbreviated as *SP*.

and André Mazon, in whose work, as later in his own, language could never be seen as something isolated but always in relation to the speakers or writers from whom alone we have knowledge of it.

The main themes which dominate Unbegaun's work are three: the Russian literary language, past and present; Russian onomastics; and the study of the other Slavonic literary languages, with Serbian occupying a place of particular importance. All these themes are already present in his earliest major publications, which belong to the 1930s, and are then developed with undiminishing originality and an ever-widening range of material in the succeeding flow of articles and monographs. To single out these three main areas is not to diminish the value of Unbegaun's contributions to other fields, for example, to bibliography,[2] and to Russian versification.[3]

2

The main thesis which gained for Unbegaun the degree of Docteur ès Lettres at Paris was a detailed study of the morphology of the noun in early sixteenth-century Russian, later published as *La Langue russe au XVIe siècle (1500–1550)*. I. *La Flexion des noms* (Bibliothèque de l'Institut français de Léningrad, xvi) (Paris, 1935). In the introduction to this work we find clearly set out the approach to the history of the Russian language which is characteristic of all Unbegaun's researches in this field: '. . . il y avait en Moscovie, à cette époque [*sc.* the sixteenth century] deux langues écrites, l'une littéraire, l'autre d'usage purement administratif. La première était le slavon; la seconde le russe de chancellerie.'[4] The uncompromising postulation of 'two languages' is fundamental to Unbegaun's conception. Proceeding from Shakhmatov's view that the Russian literary language was in origin Church Slavonic,[5] and accepting the fact that the language of legal documents was vernacular East Slavonic from the beginning, Unbegaun could not regard these two entities as 'variants', 'dialects', or 'styles' of a single language. Despite mutual influences which caused forms of the one language to influence the other under given—and definable—circumstances (especially during the period before the conservative reform of Russian

---

[2] B. O. Unbegaun (with the collaboration of J. S. G. Simmons), *A Bibliographical Guide to the Russian Language* (Oxford, 1953); B. O. Unbegaun, 'Soviet Lexicology in the Sixties' in: *Monograph Series on Languages and Linguistics*, 24 (Georgetown University School of Languages and Linguistics, 1971), 259–67; and the *Chroniques* in the *Revue des études slaves* referred to on p. 9.

[3] *Russian Versification* (Oxford, 1963).

[4] Op. cit. 5.

[5] '... по своему происхождению русский литературный язык — это перенесенный на русскую почву церковнославянский (по происхождению своему древнеболгарский) язык, в течение веков сближавшийся с живым народным языком и постепенно утративший и утрачивающий свое иноземное обличие.' A. A. Shakhmatov, *Ocherk sovremennogo russkogo literaturnogo yazyka* (M., 1925), 6–7.

Church Slavonic brought about by the 'second South Slavonic influence' of the fourteenth and fifteenth centuries), they remained separate languages. Moreover, the separation is due to a difference of function: the *literary language* is opposed to the *administrative language* (Unbegaun's term for *приказный язык*). It is perhaps noteworthy that this conception of functional languages is close to the ideas of the Prague Linguistic Circle, though the Prague conception of *langue littéraire* (translating Czech *spisovný jazyk*) is wider than that of Unbegaun: the Prague Circle opposed *langue littéraire* to *langue populaire*,[6] while for Unbegaun the important opposition was that of *langue littéraire* to *langue écrite*.[7]

The choice of the first half of the sixteenth century was justified for Unbegaun by the fact that, despite its great interest in the development of the morphological system of modern Russian the language of this period had been little studied by scholars, most of whom had not extended their detailed analyses of the history of Russian beyond the fifteenth century. The texts on which he based his study cover a wide range: legal, diplomatic, and private texts. It is noteworthy that *Domostroi* is included in the third category: there is no question of its being regarded as a text of the literary language, as it has been commonly classified by Russian scholars.

The main body of the study is a detailed analysis of the declensional forms of nominal words in the texts under review (nouns, adjectives, pronouns, numerals). The analysis is not merely descriptive; the forms occurring in the texts are explained historically and compared with later stages of the language. Thus there emerges not merely a characterization of the language of the texts studied but a dynamic portrayal of the processes which gave rise to the morphological system of modern Russian. The combination of synchrony and diachrony, which is fundamental to Unbegaun's method, is fully justified not merely by the fact that he is studying texts ranging over half a century but by the dynamism inherent in any *état de langue*. The language of any period contains at one and the same time obsolescent and productive elements. By isolating these and relating them to past and future developments it is possible to gain some impression of what the 'history' of a language means in real terms. Thus Unbegaun's monograph is something more than an analysis of the sixteenth-century texts in question; it is a most valuable manual of Russian historical morphology, supplementing and often surpassing the morphological sections of the standard historical grammars.

3

In the preface to his study of sixteenth-century Russian Unbegaun

[6] See the *Thèses* of the Prague Linguistic Circle in *Travaux du Cercle Linguistique de Prague*, 1 (Prague, 1929), especially pp. 15 ff.
[7] *La Langue russe au XVIe siècle . . .*, 5 ff.

stated that it was the first of two volumes. 'La seconde [partie],' he wrote, 'consacrée à la flexion du verbe, fera l'objet d'un volume ultérieur qui, j'espère, ne tardera pas de paraître à son tour.'[8] It is a great pity that this second volume never appeared. However, the language of Muscovy remained one of Unbegaun's main interests throughout his life. The material that he had collected for the monograph on sixteenth-century morphology, and which he supplemented from his reading in earlier and later Muscovite documents, provided an ample source for a series of studies on the Russian vocabulary. In default of a dictionary of Middle Russian the Muscovite texts offered a host of unrecorded words and of lexical problems to be solved. Characteristic of Unbegaun's work in this field are his studies on the Old Russian terms for 'rhinoceros', on personal descriptions in the Muscovite *kabal'nye knigi*, in which he gave a subtle and penetrating analysis of Old Russian colour-terms, and on the word подвойский 'bailiff', where fifteenth- and sixteenth-century evidence from Muscovy and Pskov enabled him to correct the accepted etymology of Polish *podwojski* (~ *podwój* 'gate', not ~ *wojski* 'military governor').[9]

When Unbegaun came to Oxford in the 1950s he became acquainted with a new source for the study of the language of Muscovy, one which proved to be of unusual interest and on which he based many of his later articles. This was represented by the Russian vocabularies compiled by two English travellers in Russia, Mark Ridley (1599) and Richard James (1618–20),[10] both of which are preserved in manuscript in the Bodleian Library. James's vocabulary was edited and published in Leningrad by B. A. Larin in 1959;[11] and in two articles[12] Unbegaun reviewed this edition, acknowledging its merits but also correcting a number of false readings or misinterpretations, and giving convincing explanations of points which the Russian editor had found obscure. Unbegaun's incomparable knowledge of the contemporary texts from sixteenth- and seventeenth-century Muscovy enabled him time after time to clarify James's entries and fit them into the linguistic pattern of their time. The vocabulary of Mark Ridley has not yet been edited. It was being prepared for publication by Unbegaun and Mr. J. S. G. Simmons; and this work is now being continued in Oxford. The material from this vocabulary, too, figures largely in Unbegaun's articles on

---

[8] *La Langue russe au XVIe siècle . . .*, ix.

[9] 'Wie hieß das Rhinozeros im Altrussischen?', *SP* 169–75; 'Les anciens Russes vus par eux-mêmes', ibid. 272–86; 'La fausse évidence étymologique: polonais *podwojski*, russe *podvojskij*', *Symbolae linguisticae in honorem Georgii Kuryłowicz* (Polska Akademia Nauk, Prace Komisji Językoznawstwa, 5 (Wrocław–Warsaw–Cracow, 1965), 335–9.

[10] See B. O. Unbegaun and J. S. G. Simmons, 'Slavonic Manuscript Vocabularies in the Bodleian Library', *Oxford Slavonic Papers*, ii (1951), 119–27.

[11] B. A. Larin, *Russko-angliiskii slovar'-dnevnik Richarda Dzhemsa (1618–1619 gg.)* (L., 1959).

[12] 'The Language of Muscovite Russia in Oxford Vocabularies', *SP* 237–54; 'Nablyudeniya anglichanina nad russkim yazykom kontsa XVI v.', ibid. 262–71.

historical lexicology. It was Ridley's mention of the word *этот*, together with a rudimentary declensional paradigm, that made it possible to establish convincingly that this pronoun was in normal colloquial use before 1600.[13] Ridley and James provided the earliest attestations of *матка*, the Old Russian word for 'compass',[14] as well as for the now dialectal *курпы* '(hempen) shoes' which Ridley's testimony shows to have been used in Moscow and not merely in the north-western area to which it had previously been assigned.[15] In his studies on these and a number of other words Unbegaun skilfully combined the evidence of the Oxford vocabularies with a wide and detailed knowledge of languages and of the *realia* of European civilization so that the result enriches not only etymological research but also Russian cultural history.

The Bodleian vocabularies provided a particularly striking example of the importance of the testimony of foreigners for the study of early modern Russian. Unbegaun frequently pointed to the value of such evidence: the uninformed foreigner, with no linguistic prejudices, preconceptions, or conventions to circumscribe or distort his observations, simply wrote down what he heard and thus provided the unadulterated raw material of language which is there for the philologist to exploit. The vocabularies of Ridley and James are, of course, by no means the only examples of this kind of material. Unbegaun from time to time adduces material from the manuscript vocabulary of 1607 compiled by the Low German speaker Tönnies Fenne and recently edited by Roman Jakobson together with other scholars.[16]

Another text falling into this general category to which Unbegaun attached very great importance was the Russian grammar written by the German H. W. Ludolf and published in Oxford at the University Press in 1696.[17] This first printed Russian grammar, despite some imperfections, again showed the value of the observations of foreigners, showing, in Unbegaun's words, 'a reasonable appreciation of the Russian grammatical system'.[18] The study of Ludolf led to that of other grammars written by non-Russians which antedated Lomonosov's work, those of Kopijewitz (1706), Adodurov (1731), and Groening (1750). These formed the subject of Unbegaun's paper at the Fourth International Congress of Slavists in Moscow in 1958[19] and were republished by him with a short but informative preface ten years later.[20]

---

[13] 'Das Alter von russisch *etot*', *SP* 165–8.   [14] 'Le nom de la boussole en russe', *SP* 197–202.

[15] 'Ein baltisches Lehnwort im Moskovitischen Rußland', *Die Welt der Slaven*, viii (1962), 346–9.

[16] L. L. Hammerich, R. Jakobson, *et al.* (eds.), *Tönnies Fenne's Low German Manual of Spoken Russian, Pskov 1607*, 2 vols. (Copenhagen, 1961–70).

[17] B. O. Unbegaun (ed.), *Henrici Wilhelmi Ludolfii Grammatica Russica Oxonii A.D. MDCXCVI* (Oxford, 1959).   [18] Ibid. ix.

[19] 'Russian Grammars before Lomonosov', *Oxford Slavonic Papers*, viii (1958), 98–116.

[20] *Drei russische Grammatiken des 18. Jahrhunderts. Nachdruck der Ausgaben von 1706, 1731 und 1750 mit einer Einleitung von B. O. Unbegaun* (Slavische Propyläen, 55), (Munich, 1969).

4

As was noted earlier, Unbegaun's study of sixteenth-century Russian was based on the conception of two separate languages which coexisted in the period before the eighteenth century: the East Slavonic vernacular and the imported Church Slavonic, or, in sixteenth-century terms, the administrative language and the literary language. In the last decade of his life he developed this conception in a series of articles. Deliberately provocative in their formulations, these articles aroused keen controversy, and the thesis expressed in them was the subject of sometimes dramatic debates, as at the Sixth International Congress of Slavists in Prague in 1968. The thesis was first set out at some length in an article contributed to a volume issued to commemorate the eleven-hundredth anniversary of the Cyrillo-Methodian mission. The title 'L'héritage cyrillo-méthodien en Russie'[21] leads the reader to expect a survey of the development of the Church Slavonic language, the creation of Saints Cyril and Methodius, on Russian soil. Such a survey is indeed offered but it leads to far-reaching conclusions. Unbegaun characterizes the following successive stages: the introduction of a new language for written purposes, based on a Balkan Slavonic dialect, after the Christianization of Rus'; the coexistence of this language, in the Middle Ages, with a written form of the East Slavonic vernacular which was used for legal documents and from which Church Slavonic differed essentially only in syntax and vocabulary; the divergence of the two languages after the fourteenth century owing to the conservative reform of Russian Church Slavonic and the changes which affected the morphology of the vernacular; a new *rapprochement* in the seventeenth century caused by the infiltration of vernacular morphology into Church Slavonic; a fusion of vocabulary in which Church Slavonic elements held their own but were amplified by elements from the vernacular; and finally the emergence of the modern Russian literary, and ultimately standard, language as a Russified form of Church Slavonic. This thesis was repeated with increasing emphasis and supporting arguments in the articles which followed. In his discussion of the current tasks facing students of Russian historical grammar Unbegaun defined his position with complete, and, to some, alarming, clarity:

Что же требуется от исторической грамматики русского языка, чтобы, с одной стороны, преодолеть ничем не оправдываемый разрыв в изложении истории русского языка до и после XVIII в. и, с другой стороны, подвести приемлемый исторический фундамент под современный русский литературный язык? Лишь одно: признать, что этот русский литературный язык является русифицированным церковнославянским литератур-

---

[21] In M. Hellmann *et al.* (eds.), *Cyrillo-Methodiana. Zur Frühgeschichte des Christentums bei den Slaven 863–1963*, 470–82.

ным языком, развивавшимся без перерыва, хоть и не без толчков, с XI в. до наших дней. Тогда все станет на свое место.[22]

He emphatically rejected the conception of a mere fusion of the Church Slavonic and vernacular components, a conception which allowed neither component a decisive role in the formation of modern literary Russian. 'Слияния языков не бывает', he wrote, 'как не бывает слияния рек: одна река впадает в другую, один язык поглощает другой'.[23] The 'cardinal question' was: 'Кто же кого поглотил при образовании русского литературного языка в 18 веке?'[24] This conception was unacceptable to a number of other scholars. At the Prague Congress of 1968 V. V. Vinogradov 'decisively rejected' it, opposing to it a view which saw the Russian literary language as the result of the 'interaction and synthesis' of four factors: Church Slavonic, the language of administration and law which had developed in the pre-literary period, the 'language of folklore', and dialectal elements.[25] Even Vinogradov, however, conceded to Church Slavonic the role of 'condensator and grammatical-syntactic regulator' in the early period.[26] In the same discussion Nikita Tolstoy was somewhat more sympathetic to Unbegaun's view, accepting the 'organizing role' of Church Slavonic, especially in the lexical domain.[27]

In his last years Unbegaun returned again and again to this theme. It formed the subject of his Presidential Address to the Modern Humanities Research Association in January 1973, where he expressed it in general terms and against a wide European background for the benefit of a non-specialist audience. The final paragraph of that address contains a last, uncompromising statement of his position: 'And here Modern Standard Russian stands, a naturalized alien with an uninterrupted tradition of nine hundred years, first as a Church language, then as a literary language, and, finally, as an all-purpose standard, and the spoken idiom of the educated. Such a development is unique in the Slavonic world. It is unparalleled among the languages of Europe.'[28]

The debate continues and will continue. Whether or not Unbegaun's thesis comes to be generally accepted by scholars, it has the great merit of having stimulated research into the neglected 'middle period' of the

---

[22] 'Istoricheskaya grammatika russkogo yazyka i ee zadachi', *Yazyk i chelovek* (Publikatsii Otdeleniya strukturnoi i prikladnoi lingvistiki, vyp. iv) (M., 1970), 262–7; for the passage quoted, see p. 267.

[23] 'Russkii literaturnyi yazyk: problemy i zadachi ego izucheniya' in: *Poetika i stilistika russkoi literatury. Pamyati akademika Viktora Vladimirovicha Vinogradova* (L., 1971), 329–33; for the passage quoted, see p. 331.

[24] 'Proiskhozhdenie russkogo literaturnogo yazyka', *Novyi zhurnal*, kn. 100 (New York, 1970), 306–19; for the passage quoted, see p. 311.

[25] *VI. Mezinárodní sjezd slavistů v Praze 1968. Akta sjezdu*, 2, p. 461.

[26] Ibid.   [27] Ibid. 462.

[28] 'The Russian Literary Language: a Comparative View', *Modern Language Review*, lxviii (1973), xxv.

Russian language, from the fourteenth to the eighteenth centuries. Unbegaun frequently alluded to the necessity for detailed studies of the language of this period, supplementing his own work. Such studies should, moreover, deal in particular with the as yet unwritten history of Church Slavonic in Russia. Only after studies of this kind have been carried out will it be possible to assess the correctness of Unbegaun's model of the history of the Russian literary language. The fact that they are being undertaken, in particular by Unbegaun's own pupils, is not the least important part of his legacy to scholarship.

5

Russian onomastics was one of Unbegaun's earliest scholarly interests. Already in 1929 he published a note on the name of St. Petersburg,[29] and one of his first studies to appear after the publication of his book on sixteenth-century Russian was concerned with place-names. This article, 'Les noms des villes russes: la mode slavonne',[30] derived from his concern with the opposition of Church Slavonic and vernacular elements in the Russian literary language. He showed how in the Muscovite period Church Slavonic names were almost entirely restricted to places which were named after churches, such as Blagoveshchenskoe, Uspenskoe, etc., while names of a secular character bore a vernacular form, e.g. Novgorod, Belgorod, Yur'ev. He then discussed the new place-names of the eighteenth century which came into existence largely as a result of the Russian imperial expansion to the south and east. After 1750, he showed, such names were formed with Church Slavonic elements, e.g. Ekaterinograd, Ekaterinoslav, Georgievsk, and it could even happen that an older vernacular form was replaced by a Church Slavonic one, as when the place known in the Old Russian chronicles (and still in the eighteenth century) as Volodimer was rechristened Vladimir. Although this 'mode slavonne' became less marked in the nineteenth century, it showed, in Unbegaun's view, the importance of Church Slavonic as the main constituent of the new literary Russian that was the product of the eighteenth century. A second article[31] dealt with a more aberrant form of eighteenth-century name-giving, the 'mode grecque' which gave rise to such names as Stavropol', Mariupol', Kherson, and the like. These two articles show the characteristic, which is typical of all Unbegaun's work, that the detailed study of particular phenomena points to more general principles and conclusions of very wide significance. Illuminating though the two studies are for the linguistic and cultural history of the eight-

---

[29] 'Le nom de Saint-Pétersbourg', *Revue des études slaves*, ix (1929), 272–3.
[30] *SP* 58–68.
[31] 'Les noms des villes russes: la mode grecque', *SP* 69–91.

eenth century, they also cast light on the whole development of Russian place-names from the earliest times to the Soviet period.

After 1945 Unbegaun increasingly directed his attention to Russian personal names, and in particular to surnames. His last book, and indeed his longest published work, was the magisterial study of Russian surnames which appeared in the year before his death.[32] This is the fullest study of the subject ever to appear. After a discussion of the origin and types of Russian surnames and of their morphological characteristics, over 10,000 names are classified, analysed, and placed in their historical and social context. Like all Unbegaun's other works this one, too, is not 'pure philology' but provides a host of insights into Russian life and cultural history.

6

From his student days in Ljubljana Unbegaun never ceased to cultivate an interest in the Slavonic languages other than Russian; and this interest is reflected in his publications from 1928 onwards. It was then that he began to contribute to the *Revue des études slaves* an annual bibliographical *chronique* of new publications on White Russian; this was supplemented from 1931 by a similar *chronique* on Ukrainian. For a few years after the Second World War he also supplied the *chroniques* on Sorbian, Polabian, and Kashubian. For the *thèse complémentaire* which he submitted for the doctoral degree he chose a Serbian subject. This thesis appeared in book form as *Les Débuts de la langue littéraire chez les Serbes* (Travaux publiés par l'Institut d'Études slaves, xv) (Paris, 1935). It gives an account of the development of the Serbian literary language in the eighteenth century, showing how Serbian Church Slavonic gave way, after about 1740, to Russian Church Slavonic, and how, towards the end of the century, vernacular elements penetrated more and more into the written language. The account ends on the eve of Vuk Karadžić's reforms.

In its relatively brief span of 83 pages this study gives a concise and authoritative exposition of a highly complicated subject. The unsystematic variety of the texts written by eighteenth-century Serbs had never previously been subjected to such an orderly analysis; and Unbegaun's monograph remains the most useful introduction to the subject. In the last forty years, and in particular since the Second World War, much important work has been done on the Serbian language in the period immediately preceding the advent of Vuk Karadžić,[33] and as a result of it the picture drawn by Unbegaun has been modified in detail and

---

[32] *Russian Surnames* (Oxford, 1972).

[33] See, for example, A. Mladenović, *O narodnom jeziku Jovana Rajića* (Belgrade, 1964), and the literature cited by A. Albin in *Slavonic and East European Review*, li (1973), 497–8.

emphasis. In particular, it is now clear that the influence of the popular language on writers in the Vojvodina was more widespread and far-reaching than appears from Unbegaun's account. These advances in research in no way invalidate that account which remains a minor masterpiece and a milestone in the study of the Serbo-Croatian literary language.

Three years before the appearance of his two doctoral theses Unbegaun had shown his mastery of the comparative Slavonic field in an article which, though dealing with a vast theme in a relatively brief space, represented yet another contribution of fundamental importance. This was the article on 'Le calque dans les langues slaves littéraires' which appeared in the *Revue des études slaves*, xii, in February 1932.[34] This surveyed the use of calques in eight Slavonic languages, Serbo-Croat, Slovene, Czech, Sorbian, Polish, Russian, Bulgarian, and Ukrainian. In passing there are several illuminating references to Hungarian. After surveying a mass of material illustrating the extent and manner in which calques (translation-loans) are employed in the languages discussed Unbegaun divided these languages into two classes, 'langues à calques': Croatian, Slovene, Czech, and Sorbian; and 'langues à emprunts': Polish, Russian, Serbian, and Bulgarian. Ukrainian occupied a special place: its abstract vocabulary had been largely borrowed from Polish, though Ukrainianized in form, so that the words in question might reasonably be classed either as loans or as calques. The classification is justified and Unbegaun's comments on it are highly stimulating. He associates the calque with bilingual situations and notes the importance of the phenomenon in characterizing the common features of the languages of Central Europe: 'On parle depuis longtemps de la communauté linguistique du monde balkanique, une communauté qui s'affirme par les traits généraux de vocabulaire et de syntaxe, voire de morphologie. Mais, si l'on s'attache quelque jour à déterminer une pareille communauté de l'Europe centrale, c'est le procédé du calque qui en sera l'indice le plus caractéristique.'[35] It is unfortunate that, apart from a few isolated articles, little has been done to carry forward research in this field in which Unbegaun made such an excellent start. It was characteristic of him that he was at first unwilling to approve the inclusion of 'Le calque linguistique . . .' in the volume of his selected papers but, after listening to the pleas of the editors, decided that it was 'not so bad after all'. It is true that, after more than forty years there is much detail in the article that might be modified, amplified, or corrected. But its main principles remain as stimulating and valuable as when it was written.

From about 1960 Unbegaun on several occasions returned to the comparative study of the Slavonic literary languages, of their character and relationships. This went side by side with his study of the Russian literary language which has been characterized above. Russian, in his view, was opposed to all the other Slavonic languages in that it was based on a language (or dialect) imported from abroad, whereas all the others were firmly based on native elements. The most detailed expression of his views on the Slavonic literary languages is contained in the addresses he made to the Eighth and Tenth Congresses of the International Federation of Modern Languages and Literatures (Liège, 1960 and Strasbourg, 1966).[36] One fundamental thesis is contained in the first sentence of the Liège lecture: 'Chaque langue littéraire est fondée sur un dialecte déterminé.' A second asserts that the unity of the Slavonic languages is most clearly expressed in the basic elements of the lexicon, their diversity in the higher or abstract vocabulary: '. . . dans les langues romanes, l'unité est en haut, la diversité est en bas. Dans les langues slaves, l'unité est en bas, la diversité est en haut. Il s'ensuit qu'il est illusoire de poser un principe unique de la formation et encore moins du développement des langues littéraires slaves, puisque ces langues participent à des aires culturelles différentes.'[37] A third frequently repeated theme is the demand for clarity of terminology in the study of 'literary languages'. While at the present day it is reasonable to employ the term 'literary language' as synonymous with 'standard language' this is a state of affairs which dates only from the nineteenth century. For earlier periods a careful and systematic choice of terms is necessary so that we may know precisely what is being discussed and that comparisons may have meaning.[38]

There can be little disagreement with the second and third of these propositions. The comparison between the Slavonic and Romance languages is illuminating; and lack of clarity and uniformity of terminology has indeed led to many misunderstandings and misleading statements in studies of the Slavonic literary languages. A clarification of categories and terms for the periods before 1750 would be highly desirable not only for Russian but also for the other Slavonic languages. It is, however, difficult to give full assent to Unbegaun's dogmatic statement that every literary language is based on a single dialect. This is indeed true of Czech, of Serbo-Croat as it developed after 1850, and of many other languages, Slavonic or non-Slavonic. But there are also doubtful cases. It is difficult to define the *dialecte déterminé* which lies at the basis of modern standard Slovak, unless we use the term 'dialect' in

[36] 'La formation des langues littéraires slaves: problèmes et état des questions', *Langue et littérature. Actes du VIIIe Congrès de la Fédération internationale des Langues et Littératures modernes* (Bibliothèque de la Faculté de Philosophie et Lettres de l'Université de Liège, fasc. clxi) (Paris, 1961), 134–46; 'Les contacts culturels des langues slaves', *Le Réel dans la littérature et dans la langue. Actes du Xe Congrès de la Fédération internationale des Langues et Littératures modernes (F.I.L.L.M.) Strasbourg (29 août — 3 septembre 1966): Actes et Colloques*, 6 (Paris, 1967), 123–36.
[37] 'La formation . . .' (n. 36), 136.   [38] Ibid. 139 f.

a much wider and vaguer sense than is usual.[39] Slovene, moreover, simply cannot be fitted into Unbegaun's definition. This is a literary language which can only be analysed as the result of a mixture of dialects.[40] The mixture can be explained historically but we cannot isolate 'un dialecte déterminé' as being of cardinal importance in the historical process. One might also instance Hungarian as a literary language resulting from a mixture of dialects. One of Unbegaun's greatest gifts was to see the elements of order in apparently chaotic material, and to devise principles which enabled the detached observer to isolate the tendencies and processes of linguistic development. In this one instance he allowed himself to oversimplify the facts.

7

This review of Unbegaun's scholarly achievement has concentrated on the central themes of his work. Much more could be said of his writings on Russian grammar[41] and versification,[42] on his contribution to Old Russian textology,[43] to Rumanian etymology,[44] and much else besides. It is nevertheless in his contributions to the study of the Russian literary language, of Russian onomastics, and of the development and connections of the Slavonic literary languages in general that we can best see the brilliance and originality of his scholarship.

[39] See the present writer's article 'Dialect, κοινή, and tradition in the formation of literary Slovak', *Slavonic and East European Review*, xxxix (1961), 339–45.

[40] See the present writer's article 'The formation of the Slovene literary language against the background of the Slavonic national revival', *Slavonic and East European Review*, xli (1963), 391–402.

[41] Especially his *Russian Grammar* (Oxford, 1957).

[42] See n. 3.

[43] 'Les relations vieux-russes de la prise de Constantinople', *SP* 1–26.

[44] 'Les noms de la neige en roumain', *SP* 148–53.

An Unpublished Epigram on an English Ambassador to Russia

By J. LURIA (Ya. S. LUR'E)

THE subject of 'Muscovy' occupied a considerable place in English literature of the sixteenth and seventeenth centuries. 'Muscovites' are mentioned in the plays of Shakespeare (*Love's Labour's Lost* and *The Winter's Tale*) and Heywood; the action of one of John Fletcher's plays takes place in Moscow; Russian words are used for puns in a pamphlet by Thomas Nashe; the poet George Turberville, who went to Russia with Randolph's mission, wrote letters in verse from Moscow.[1] It is interesting to observe how Anglo-Russian relations are also indirectly reflected in the literatures of both countries: for example, the visit to England of the Italian duke Virginio Orsini in the winter of 1600–1 prompted Shakespeare to make him one of the main characters in *Twelfth Night* which was produced at that time, while on 6 January 1601, on the very eve of Twelfth Night, the Russian ambassadors Mikulin and Zinov'ev met the same 'Prince Verdzhen Aursinov' at a royal reception and mentioned him in their official report (*stateinyi spisok*). This report of Mikulin and Zinov'ev also contained details of another event which seriously affected Shakespeare and his theatre, namely the insurrection of Essex. Among the supporters of Essex listed by the Russian envoys in their report were a number of people closely connected with Shakespeare.[2] The reflection of Anglo-Russian relations in the literature of the sixteenth and seventeenth centuries is a subject which warrants special study.

The purpose of this article is to draw attention to a hitherto unknown literary text connected with the history of diplomatic relations between the two countries at the end of the sixteenth century—a short poem written in the margin of a copy of *Purchas his Pilgrimage* in the main collection of the Library of the Academy of Sciences of the U.S.S.R. in Leningrad.[3] This edition of Purchas, published in 1626, belonged at

---

[1] See M. P. Alekseev, 'Angliiskii yazyk v Rossii i russkii yazyk v Anglii', *Uchenye zapiski Leningradskogo gos. universiteta*, lxxii, *Seriya filologicheskikh nauk*, ix (1944), 80–1; idem, 'Shekspir i russkoe gosudarstvo XVI–XVII vv.' in: *Shekspir i russkaya kul'tura* (M.–L., 1965), 784–805. See also K. Ruffmann, *Das Russlandbild im England Shakespeares* (Göttingen, 1952).

[2] *Puteshestviya russkikh poslov XVI–XVII vv.* (M.–L., 1954), 176, 179–80.

[3] *Purchas his Pilgrimage, or Relations of the World and the Religions observed in all Ages and Places Discovered, from the Creation unto this Present*, 4 ed. (London, 1626). Biblioteka Akademii nauk shelf-mark: $\frac{\text{IX Pc}}{\text{IV}}$.

one time to the East India Company ('Comitee of Warehouses of the Honble. East India Company, N 58'[4]); the person, or one of the persons, who made notes in the margins left his signature in the book: 'Doyly Michel'.[5] There was a professional soldier of that name in the seventeenth century: Michael Doyly (or D'Oylie), son of Thomas D'Oylie, the distinguished scholar who compiled *Bibliotheca Hispanica*.[6] Purchas's book, a continuation of Hakluyt's *Principal Navigations*, contains a number of accounts of foreign countries, among them 'Extracts out of Sir Jerome Horseys Observations in seventeen yeeres travels and experience in Russia and other countries adjoining'. In these extracts there is mention of the arrival in Russia in 1583–4 of the English ambassador Sir Jerome Bowes. In the margin of p. 982, next to a sidenote which reads 'Sir Jer. Bowes Embassadour into Russia', there is a manuscript note, which has been partly trimmed away in binding: '. . . verses . . . made . . . him'.[7] Below this, in the tail margin, is the text of a poem which runs as follows (the original spelling has been retained, but the text has been divided into lines):

> God made men; & men made mony.
> God made bees; & bees made hony.
> God made owles, & apes, & asses:
> God made Sir Jerome Bowes, & S[r] Jerome Bowes made Glasses.

This is followed by a note in prose: 'Be [evidently in error for 'He'] brought in th[a]t art but was ruind by it'.

As far as we can tell, this poem is unknown to scholars and has never been published before. It is not unlike the still extant nursery rhyme:

> God made the bees
> And the bees make honey,
> The miller's man does all the work,
> But the miller makes the money.[8]

When was this poem about Bowes written and in what connection? The notes in the margins of Purchas's book were made not earlier than the middle of the seventeenth century: one of them, in the margin of a passage towards the end of the extract from Horsey's *Observations* in which Mikhail Fedorovich Romanov's accession is described, mentions the death of Tsar Mikhail in 1649.[9] However, it seems very unlikely

[4] *Purchas his Pilgrimage*, title page.
[5] Ibid. head margin, above the dedication to the Archbishop of Canterbury (page not numbered).
[6] *DNB*, v (1908), 1323.
[7] It is likely that the full text read: '[these] verses [were] made [upon] him.'
[8] L. Untermeyer, *The Golden Treasury of English Poetry* (New York, 1959), 29. I am grateful to Mr. J. S. G. Simmons for pointing this out to me and also for suggesting the wording of the note proposed in n. 7.
[9] *Purchas his Pilgrimage* (n. 3), 992. 'Hee dyed, 1649'—the note comes at the end of the text.

either that the poem quoted above was written in the middle of the seventeenth century or that it can be attributed, for instance, to the Michael Doyly who left his signature in the book and who probably lived at about this time. By the mid seventeenth century Sir Jerome Bowes was long since dead (he died in 1616),[10] and there would have been little point in writing epigrams on him at that time. Whoever made the marginal notes in Purchas's book evidently recalled some 'verses' which had been written during Bowes's lifetime and which, like any other epigram, were both topical and witty. In 1592 Jerome Bowes did in fact obtain a patent for the manufacture of glass in England, and the undertaking was a failure.[11] But it is doubtful whether the failure of Bowes's enterprise was implied in the epigram, which remained for half a century in the memory of whoever read the account of Bowes's diplomatic activity.[12] That the author was clearly ill-disposed towards Bowes can be seen from the choice of animals with which he compares him (owls, apes, asses), and this hostility can hardly be justified simply by the shortcomings of Bowes's business acumen. We must seek a deeper reason.

The most reliable clue to the meaning of the epigram on Bowes is provided by the contents of the book in the margins of which it is found. Horsey's *Observations*, as included in Purchas's *Pilgrimage*, mention Bowes's arrival in Russia, the ambassador's capricious behaviour,[13] the mortal danger which threatened Bowes in Russia after the death of Ivan the Terrible, and Horsey's intercession on his behalf.[14] Further on in his narrative Horsey mentions an intrigue hatched against him by Bowes several years later when he, Horsey, arrived in England in 1586 with various diplomatic commissions from the Tsar. '[I omit] the imputations and aspersions cast on me by false suggestions and subornations of Finch, a hang-by of Sir Jerome Bowes, who first faltered, and after the other being removed out of presence [of the Queen], confessed that he was set on by him; I omit, so repaying the courtesie in releasing him when he had beene taken as a Spie, etc.'[15] The full text of Horsey's narrative—it is considerably abridged in Purchas's version—reveals the true nature of the intrigue which Bowes had hatched: Bowes had tried to cause a rift between Horsey on the one hand and the Queen and Leicester on the other by accusing Horsey of reporting 'to divers dukes

---

[10] *DNB*, ii (1908), 966.

[11] W. H. Price, *The English Patents of Monopoly* (London–Boston, 1906), 70–1.

[12] There is another possible interpretation of the last line of the epigram: in the sixteenth and early seventeenth centuries 'glasse' ('glasses') was an alternative spelling of 'glosse', 'glosses' (see *OED*, s.v. *glass* sb.¹, sense 13, and the example there quoted: 'the more shamefull facts he leadeth us unto, the more goodly glasse he setteth on them' (1569)). Could not this be a pun and might not the epigram contain a hint of Bowes's activity as a political intriguer?

[13] *Purchas his Pilgrimage* (n. 3), 983.

[14] Ibid. 984–5.

[15] Ibid. 987.

and noblemen how that he [Leicester] had cast his wiff down a pare of stares, braek her naeck, and so became the Quens minion'[16]—an accusation all the more piquant for the fact that nine years earlier Bowes himself had been in trouble for slandering Leicester.[17] Bowes's attempt to 'break Horsey's neck' did not meet with success; in a side-note to Purchas's text we read of the failure of Finch and Bowes: 'One was committed to the Marshall, the other forbidden her Majesties presence'.[18]

The significance of this conflict between Bowes and Horsey is more serious than we are usually led by historians to believe. When examining the activities of Horsey in Russia and in particular his conflict with Bowes, Russian historians have usually explained all these facts by purely personal motives—Horsey's immorality and 'egoism', Bowes's arrogance, etc.; the English historian Charles Sisson interprets Horsey's activity in the same way.[19] There is, however, sufficient evidence to enable us to see the conflict between Horsey and Bowes as political in character: Horsey was the protégé of Secretary of State Walsingham, who favoured a firm anti-Spanish policy and broad international political alliances; Bowes, on the other hand, was linked with the party at court which advocated a 'cautious' foreign policy—the party headed by Lord Treasurer Burghley and Lord Chamberlain Hunsdon. In the course of unofficial negotiations in Russia he expressed the views of this group, boasting of Elizabeth's non-interference in the religious conflict of the Netherlands and France. Meanwhile Horsey and his colleagues intercepted the correspondence of the Spanish agent in Russia, Jan de Valle, interfered with the course of Russian-Spanish negotiations, and even planned to seize Spanish ships in Russian waters.[20] The underlying political cause of the conflict between Horsey and Bowes was also revealed at the time of the above-mentioned clash of 1586. According to Horsey, two of the most powerful political figures of the age, Hunsdon and Walsingham, were directly involved in this conflict: 'The lord chamberleyne hied him from the lordes to the Quen; Mr. Secretarie

---

[16] *Russia at the Close of the XVIth Century*, ed. E. A. Bond (1856), 215. In Purchas's work the text of Horsey's *Observations*, which was not published in full until the nineteenth century, was edited and abridged throughout. Various remarks about Bowes which were in Horsey's original work (see ibid. 198–9, 202–3) were considerably toned down in Purchas's version.

[17] *Calendar of State Papers, Domestic, Addenda, 1566–1579* (1871), 517 (summary of a letter dated 8 August 1577).

[18] *Purchas his Pilgrimage* (n. 3), 987.

[19] See Yu. Tolstoy, *Pervye 40 let snoshenii mezhdu Rossieyu i Anglieyu* (Spb., 1875), 39–49; C. J. Sisson, 'Englishmen in Shakespeare's Muscovy or The Victims of Jerome Horsey' in: *Mélanges en honneur de Jules Legras* (Paris, 1939).

[20] See Ya. S. Lur'e, 'Angliiskaya politika na Rusi v kontse XVI v.', *Uchenye zapiski Leningradskogo gos. pedagogicheskogo inst. im. Gertsena*, lxi (L., 1947), 129–30, 135–6; idem, 'Russko-angliiskie otnosheniya i mezhdunarodnaya politika vtoroi poloviny XVI v.', in *Mezhdunarodnye svyazi Rossii do XVII v.* (M., 1961), 434–42 (English summary, 443).

[Walsingham] gott an other waye before him, told her Majesty what had paste. She blamed my lord Honsden . . .'.[21]

At the end of the sixteenth and the beginning of the seventeenth century the advocates of a 'cautious' foreign policy gained the upper hand over those who followed Walsingham's firm line; and in spite of the failure of his plot against Horsey in 1586 and in spite of yet another scandal—he was accused of forging a will[22]—Jerome Bowes resumed his diplomatic career at the beginning of the seventeenth century: in 1600 1 he was receiving the Russian envoys who had arrived in London. Horsey, on the other hand, gave up his diplomatic activity during this period and we find him in the ranks of the parliamentary opposition to the Queen's policy;[23] at the same time the book on Muscovy written by Horsey's patron Giles Fletcher was banned—officially because of Fletcher's sharp remarks about the Russian tsar, but in fact probably because of the general anti-absolutist position of the author.[24]

In the middle of the seventeenth century, at the time of the Great Rebellion, the situation altered. In spite of the fact that after the execution of King Charles in 1649 the government of Aleksey Mikhailovich broke off diplomatic relations with the English Commonwealth, the political leaders of the Commonwealth, seeking for allies in their struggle with the papists, displayed a keen interest in the distant State of Russia. Fletcher's book, the anti-absolutist tendencies of which could now no longer be considered objectionable, was once more authorized; a special work on Muscovy was written by one of the foremost political figures of the Republic, Milton. It was in these circumstances that one of the readers of Horsey's story called to mind the epigram which reflected the old clash between the two Englishmen who had once pursued their diplomatic careers in Russia.

[21] *Russia at the Close of the XVIth Century* (n. 16), 217.

[22] *Calendar of State Papers, Domestic, 1581–1590* (1865), 448.

[23] *Sbornik Russkogo istoricheskogo obshchestva*, xxxviii (1883), 341; *Calendar of State Papers, Domestic, 1619–1623* (1858), 404.

[24] *Russia at the Close of the XVIth Century* (n. 16), cxxii. There are interesting references indicating that Giles Fletcher had some connection with the Essex affair at the beginning of the seventeenth century (ibid. cxxiv–cxxv).

The Empress and the Vinerian Professor:

Catherine II's Projects of Government Reforms and Blackstone's *Commentaries*

By MARC RAEFF

ON 4 August 1776 Catherine II wrote from Tsarskoe Selo to her faithful correspondent in Paris, Baron Grimm:

> Sir Blackstone qui ne m'a point envoyé ses commentaires, jouit seul de l'honneur d'être lu par S. M. depuis deux ans; oh, ses commentaires et moi, nous sommes inséparables; c'est un fournisseur de choses et d'idées inépuisable; je ne fais rien de ce qu'il y a dans son livre, mais c'est mon [un?] fil que je dévide à ma façon.[1]

In saying this the Empress was giving a good description of her working habits with respect to legislation and administration. She read voraciously and widely, and she always read with pen in hand. Not only did she make extensive excerpts and summaries of what she was reading, but she also noted her own reactions and ideas as she went along.

In the case of *Commentaries on the Laws of England* by William Blackstone (Vinerian Professor of Law in the University of Oxford, 1758–62) we are fortunate in having the full text of the notes Catherine took while reading the French translation of this classic of English jurisprudence.[2] These notes were used by her as she worked on plans for judicial reform and on drafts for new codes of civil law and procedures.[3] Together the notes and drafts allow us to glimpse the Empress at work and to gain an insight into her plans for the central government and for Russian society. The purpose of the present essay is to present the highlights of these plans and to offer some comments on the character of Catherine's views on the internal problems of Russia in the second half of her reign.

From the outset Catherine makes it clear that she is not going to study foreign law—in this case England's—in order to transfer it directly to Russia, 'Il est plus utile d'étudier les lois de sa patrie que les lois des

---

[1] 'Pis'ma Ekateriny II k Grimmu', ed. Ya. Grot, no. 34, *Sbornik Imperatorskogo Russkogo istoricheskogo obshchestva (SIRIO)*, xxiii (1878), 52.

[2] Manuscript Division, Lenin State Library, Moscow, *fond* 222, *karton* xvii, no. 1—hereafter cited as 'Notes'. For a description of these notes and details of the translation used, see Appendix A.

[3] Central State Archives of Ancient Charters (TsGADA), *razryad* x, *delo* 17—hereafter 'Drafts'. See Appendix B.

pays étrangers', she paraphrases Blackstone.[4] But the English jurist provides her with the necessary stimulus and inspiration. In the foot-steps of Blackstone, and following her own practice of using history and 'philology' for national glorification, Catherine endeavours to find in Russia historical precedents and parallels for the early English legal and institutional forms described in the *Commentaries*.[5] She assumes a connection between the Saxons and the Slavs, so that to her mind all Saxon traditions are in fact also Slavonic ones.[6] To prove her point she engages in some rather fanciful popular etymology with the intention of enhancing the native Russian tradition and placing it in the main-stream of European development.[7] In passing it may also be noted that in several instances where Blackstone emphasizes English historical antecedents, Catherine not only omits the specific English example but phrases her notes in such a way as to imply a universal historical trend.[8] Furthermore, possibly because of her German background and early upbringing, she stresses the northern European affinities, contrasting the traditions of freedom of the 'liberty-loving' Germanic and Slavonic peoples with the slavery and tyranny of the Romans as displayed in Roman law.[9]

If Catherine's historicism exemplifies her traditional Enlightenment attitudes, it may seem rather surprising that in her notes on Blackstone she invariably omits the references he makes to natural law.[10] The

---

[4] Notes, f. 1ᵛ. Cf. *Commentaires*, i (Discours préliminaire), 5–6 and 4th Oxford ed. (1770) of the *Commentaries*, i, 5–6. Quotations from the Notes and Drafts in this article are given in French where Catherine used French and in English translation where the original text is in Russian. The spelling of the French and of transliterated Russian words has, where necessary, been corrected and modernized.

[5] On this intellectual stance in eighteenth-century Russia, see H. Rogger, *National Consciousness in Eighteenth-Century Russia* (Cambridge, Mass., 1960), especially ch. iii.

[6] For example: 'Le Saxon descendait des Slavons, les manoirs sont aussi anciens que *usad'by, gospodskii dom, gospodskii dvor, gospodskie lyudi*' (Notes, f. 35). And 'NB The origin of the word baron seems to be taken from the word *bary* or *boyary*. England was settled and conquered by the Saxons who are of the race (*rod*) of Slavs' (ibid. f. 107). Cf. also Notes, f. 22ᵛ and Drafts, ff. 386, 464.

[7] 'In Mexico, Peru, Chile there is a large number of Slavonic words in the names of towns and settlements, such as, for example, the town of Cuzco (Kusko), the town of Guatemala (Gatimalo), etc., and perhaps England and America itself had the Slavs as their lawgivers, hence the similarity of institutions' (Notes, f. 108). See also Notes, ff. 32, 34, 109, and 217ᵛ.

[8] e.g. Notes, f. 66ᵛ.

[9] In connection with a description of the practices of Admiralty Courts (*Commentaires*, iv, 173): 'NB Taken from Roman law and similar to its [Rome's] customs rather than to Anglo-Saxon, wherein the spirit of freedom is more noticeable than in Roman ones, [the latter] serving to enslavement and debasement'; and with reference to the Loi d'Oléron: 'NB This is a Norman right and smells of the Slavonic North' (Notes, f. 135ᵛ). Cf. also Drafts, f. 386 ('slavery is a Tartar gift') and Notes f. 120ᵛ.

[10] The one specific reference to natural law is not taken from Blackstone: 'Natural rights [*sic*] are not subject to elimination or weakening either by time or by regulations' (Notes, f. 14). If this expresses Catherine's sincere opinion it would put her squarely in the camp of enlightened thinkers, but she may have been merely expressing a *lieu commun* without thinking of its implications.

reason for the omission might be that these ideas were accepted as a matter of course. But it seems more plausible to suppose that the omissions are deliberate and reflect the Empress's reluctance to base practice on doctrinaire juridical ideologies at the expense of the empirical and the pragmatic.

Catherine is nothing if not empirical, constantly on the look-out for the possibility of anchoring both her thoughts and actions on Russian reality, history, and practice. As she reads Blackstone she reminds herself to check on relevant Russian legislation or precedents, especially if they have a bearing on an eighteenth-century problem.[11] She duly notes similarities and especially comparisons favourable to her own administrative arrangements or legislative measures. In her draft codes she is even more explicit in reminding herself to check the existing legislation and to seek information on earlier practices and relevant legal traditions.[12] In short, these notes on her reading and on her plans for codification reveal her as completely undogmatic, with a clear sense of the practical and the possible, and with an insatiable appetite for information and stimulation from any source.[13] The Empress obviously has a bent towards syncretism—perhaps not always the most desirable intellectual orientation, but quite useful in a ruler and more effective in the long run than rigid ideological or theoretical dogmatism. Furthermore—and this is not the least important observation that our sources allow us to make—Catherine took her *métier de roi* very seriously, displaying tremendous application and industry, and doing her utmost to fulfil the role of monarch as she understood it. The time and care she devoted to reading and digesting Blackstone and to writing innumerable drafts for legislation and codification, are most impressive, especially if we recall the amount of time she spent on public and court functions, love-affairs, and cultural interests.

As Catherine read the wide-ranging description of English social organization and legal life which Blackstone gives in his *Commentaries*, she could not fail to be reminded of the social and administrative problems which plagued her empire. She recorded some of her reflections in marginal notes or in comments *à propos* of what Blackstone wrote about England. Not surprisingly she took the existing official social structure of Russia (as defined in her own laws) for granted as some-

---

[11] Notes, f. 27 ('NB Consulter les Loix de Russie sur tout cela'), 34ᵛ, 218, 352 ('NB Il faudrait comparer les loix d'Henri I Roi d'Angleterre avec celles de Iaroslav').

[12] Drafts, f. 480ᵛ ('NB See *Ustav blagochiniya* and project of new criminal code and printed *ukaz* of Aleksey Mikhailovich to forgive those who show contrition and *Tainaya ekspeditsiya* [acts]'.)

[13] Letter to Grimm from Tsarskoe Selo, 28 August 1776: 'Je me suis toujours senti [sic] beaucoup de penchant à me laisser mener par les gens qui en savent plus que moi, pourvu qu'ils ne me fassent pas sentir qu'ils en ont l'envie ou la prétention, car alors je m'enfuis à toutes jambes' ('Pis'ma Ekateriny . . .' (n. 1), 57). This may explain the failure of Diderot and Mercier de la Rivière to be taken seriously by Catherine.

thing not requiring fundamental change.[14] That is why she pays no specific attention to the bourgeois, urban aspects of English society and refers to the status of the British nobility (and gentry) only when she equates feudal (knightly) tenure with *pomest'e*. It is clear that Catherine fully accepts the basic hereditary and privileged character of the nobility, but with respect to the Russian nobility she is also very conscious of their service status.[15] Most of the significant privileges that the nobility enjoy are the result of its members' position as servants of the state. She makes a curious remark about the class being divided into six groups or categories—obviously on the basis of their service status.[16] But she is very concerned about the shaky economic position of the nobility; she knows and worries about the impoverishment of families as a result of the fragmentation of the inheritance with each successive generation. In order to restrict the deleterious consequences of this practice, Catherine proposes two measures. In the first place, real estate holdings of fewer than fifteen or twenty households should not be divided, but pass intact to one legal heir, while movable property might be split up among all heirs.[17] In the second place—obviously imitating the feudal practice of primogeniture and entail—Catherine proposes the creation of entailed estates for families with large properties—one son (presumably the eldest) inheriting the whole estate undivided, while his siblings share in the movables.[18] The family remains prosperous while many of its members are freed for activities useful to the state or to society. Of course, as Catherine is well aware, the idea had occurred to Peter the Great, who in 1714 tried to introduce single inheritance; but, as was also well known, it did not work and Catherine hopes that her efforts might be more successful since Russian society had matured and her legislation had secured the nobility's economic interests.

The Empress pays only slight attention to the needs and problems of the clergy, who—characteristically—are not considered as an estate of the realm, although they were a closed and hereditary *chin* or *soslovie*. This is not surprising, for Catherine had secularized church lands and was little inclined to give preferential treatment to a class that, in her opinion, played no major useful role in the state. But, in keeping with her desire to regularize all estate (class) organizations, she promoted the even distribution of competent parish clergy and regularized their appointment by village communities and estate owners. Inspired perhaps

[14] Drafts, f. 226–226^v; Notes ff. 21^v, 22.

[15] Notes, f. 33.

[16] Ibid. f. 21^v ('K chinam privyazana dolzhnost'') and Drafts, f. 226.

[17] Notes, ff. 27^v, 42^v, 46^v—a similar rule was to apply to state peasants (ibid. f. 47^v).

[18] With reference to *Commentaires*, iii, 27, she notes: 'The first [in a family] to be distinguished by a title has permission—for the upkeep of the title—to separate out a patrimony of 500 to 700 households which will remain in the family undivided for the oldest in the family' (Notes, f. 44).

by Blackstone's description of ecclesiastical benefices, she proposes to give local landowners—if they are so inclined and have suitable candidates—the power of nomination to parish livings, subject to confirmation by the bishops who would vouch for the theological and ecclesiastical suitability of the candidates.[19] She also suggests that for the sake of equalization and greater efficiency dioceses should coincide territorially with provinces (*gubernii*) and receive a uniform monetary allowance sufficient for their upkeep.[20] Catherine insists that the clergy should be well trained, and also proposes that the communities of state peasants should play a part in supervising the economy of the parish and have a say in the selection of their clergy.[21] Although Catherine did little to improve the ecclesiastical administration and schools, the second half of her reign witnessed a steady growth in the number of better-trained clergymen and a significant rise in their cultural level— developments that paved the way for the more active role played by children of the clergy in the Russian bureaucracy and in cultural life in the nineteenth century.[22]

Not unnaturally, the condition of the state peasantry caused the Empress to give serious consideration to their situation, and she makes some interesting proposals for the reshaping of their communal relationships. Unlike the private serfs (and similar groups) who were entirely under the control and in the care of the nobility, a situation that Catherine had no wish to change, the state peasants—about half of the peasant population—were very much the concern of the government. Although Catherine and her advisers never expressed it explicitly, it may be fairly assumed that they were well aware that any organizational and economic change in the situation of the state peasants would not only affect the condition of all serfs but also have a direct influence on the future economic development of the empire. Catherine worked out a scheme for administering the state peasants as part of the general provincial administration. This scheme was largely implemented in the *guberniya* of Ekaterinoslav in 1787 and resulted in a greater degree of order and self-government in the state peasant communities.[23] But as usual, the administrative apparatus was too cumbersome and bureaucratic for the low level of the peasants' economic development; in the event it proved unworkable, though some of its features were later

---

[19] Notes, ff. 7, 21ᵛ; Drafts, f. 225ᵛ. In so doing she is reverting to seventeenth-century practice.

[20] She suggests allocating 22,000 roubles for every *guberniya* of 300,000 to 400,000 souls. See Notes, f. 21 and Drafts, f. 225ᵛ.

[21] Notes, f. 21.

[22] See G. L. Freeze, 'The Russian Parish Clergy: Vladimir Province in the 18th Century' (dissertation, Columbia University, 1972).

[23] Notes, f. 19–19ᵛ; *Polnoe sobranie zakonov Rossiiskoi imperii*, xxii (Spb., 1830), no. 16,603 (December 1787).

incorporated in the projected reforms of the administration of state peasants put forward in the reigns of Alexander I and Nicholas I.[24]

Catherine's proposals for the rural estate, made in connection with Blackstone's discussion of tenures and titles by inheritance and of alienation by special customs, provide for a fairly comprehensive scheme of economic organization for the state peasantry. The scheme relates to one of Catherine's fundamental concerns: the encouragement of economic enterprise by protecting the property of those who are economically productive. In Catherine's project the peasant communities distribute the land in such fashion that provided a peasant works his land satis-factorily, he cannot be deprived of it.[25] The industrious and successful peasant may even bequeath his allotment to his widow and sons, with the same proviso as in the case of the nobility, namely that very small holdings should not be divided.[26] If, however, the peasant neglects his land and duties, he will, upon proper certification by the community, be deprived of his allotment, which will be apportioned to more deserving villagers.[27] The peasant communities constitute units whose members are responsible for each other, but whose assemblies and elected elders enjoy a fair amount of independence of action.[28] The basic administrative and judicial framework, however, was that of the Instructions to the Economic Administration (or *ekonomicheskii ustav*) which suffered from the usual Russian imperial disease: over-bureaucratization and mistrust of local authorities.[29] There is little question that had it been implemented, Catherine's plan would have organized the state peasantry as a rural estate, paralleling in many ways the basic safeguards of property and the limited degree of corporate self-government enjoyed by the nobility and the townspeople under the Charters of 1785. It was no doubt due to Catherine's indecisiveness and caution that none of the economic provisions were included in the 1787 draft of an administrative 'charter' for the state peasants.[30]

It was natural that Blackstone's *Commentaries*, the first modern complete and systematic exposition of the common law, should concentrate on civil law since this was the field of law most relevant to the expanding economy and social transformation of eighteenth-century England. This aspect of law attracted Catherine's attention too, but her notes

[24] See N. M. Druzhinin, *Gosudarstvennye krest'yane i reforma P. D. Kiseleva*, i (M.–L., 1946), ch. ii.

[25] Notes, ff. 47^v, 61.

[26] Ibid. ff. 35^v, 61–61^v.

[27] Ibid. ff. 35^v–36. The peasant household and allotments are to consist of the following seven categories: tilled land, meadow-land and hay, cattle, buildings, forests, water, people.

[28] Ibid. ff. 38, 61.

[29] *Polnoe sobranie zakonov Rossiiskoi imperii*, xix (Spb., 1830), no. 13,590 (4 April 1771); largely repeated in no. 16,603 (see n. 23).

[30] 'Proekt imperatritsy Ekateriny II ob ustroistve svobodnykh sel'skikh obyvatelei', *SIRIO*, xx (1877), 447–98.

and comments reveal a greater understanding of questions of administrative and social structure than of civil and procedural law; the Empress had neither the training nor the knowledge to make expert judgements on legal technicalities. Furthermore, the English model appeared to open up some new horizons for Catherine—the legal forms of capitalist economic relationships, such as torts, contracts, bankruptcy —and she was tempted simply to copy it. This probably explains why in reading Book II 'Of the Rights of Things' and Books III and IV on private and public wrongs affecting property, she merely follows closely Blackstone's text, without making any comment (except for frequent 'NBs') or excursuses of her own.[31]

On matters of civil law most of her attention is directed towards the rules of inheritance and the types of titles to property.[32] In trying to apply Blackstone's ideas she is handicapped by her obviously vague understanding of the distinctions made by English and Russian legal definitions. She distinguishes only movable and immovable property, while Blackstone speaks of personal and real property and of corporeal and incorporeal hereditaments.[33] The whole question of incorporeal hereditaments—perhaps of little importance in such an underdeveloped economy as Russia's—is left out of consideration by Catherine. In line with Russian legal practice she distinguishes clearly between inherited and acquired real property. She plans to maintain this distinction even after transfer to another generation, which means treating inherited patrimony differently from all other acquired property.[34] If enacted, this principle would naturally tend to favour fixed property relationships and discourage fluidity and the 'mobilization' of real estate for purposes of economic development. In fact one notices throughout Catherine's notes and drafts a constant tension between the need to secure permanently the economic base of the landowning population (primarily the nobility, of course, but the state peasantry would also have benefited from her proposals) and the desire to mobilize all resources for purposes of expansion. This is well illustrated by her attitude towards wills. She strongly condemns what she understands as the latitude given by English law to testamentary dispositions at the expense of the 'automatic' effect of traditional laws of inheritance.[35] This is a development she wants to prevent in Russia; but to do so means restricting the free disposal of potential assets in the form of land

[31] e.g. with respect to *Commentaires*, iv, ch. viii in Notes, ff. 137–47, where the French text of pp. 220–3 is literally copied with 'NBs' on every line.

[32] Catherine excerpts very carefully Book III, ch. xxx, xxxi.

[33] Notes, f. 30ᵛ with reference to Blackstone, Book II, ch. ii ('Corporeal Hereditaments'), and ibid. f. 154 for the expression of her confusion.

[34] Ibid. f. 36ᵛ.

[35] Ibid. f. 164ᵛ ('NB England is in such a situation now that, as a result of the unlimited will of testators, succession laws [rights] have been completely eradicated . . .'). The same sentence is repeated as a marginal comment in Drafts, f. 414ᵛ.

or some other property. Yet, perhaps not altogether consistently, she does not want the state to be in control of the disposition and ultimate fate of landed estates either. Thus she suggests that instead of an estate escheating, as it did in Russian law, on extinction of the fourth generation in direct line, it should pass on to a collateral line.[36] This would help impoverished branches of prominent families and also increase the number of moderately prosperous persons, who are the more desirable and active elements in the population.[37]

Catherine was also concerned about those aspects of legal procedure that guaranteed titles, secured property rights, and provided for speedy and equitable settlements of disputes. But in her notes she advances few concrete proposals of her own and contents herself with detailed and accurate summaries from Blackstone's chapters dealing with torts and bankruptcy procedures. In her draft codes she copies these excerpts word for word. To facilitate speedy settlements and rapid checking of titles she suggests decentralizing the procedures of registration and record keeping. Most records of transactions affecting property and contracts should be kept in provincial centres and claims should be made within reasonable time.[38] Of course, because of Russia's size, longer periods must be allowed for claims and contestations than in England where everything can be done through London and within a short time.[39]

In criminal matters she repeats her opposition to torture[40] and also suggests more flexible and generous provisions for bail and sureties so as not to keep defendants in jail needlessly.[41] One may say that this would only benefit members of the propertied classes, since only they were able to put up bail or find relatives or friends willing and able to act as surety for their appearance in court.

Finally, it should be mentioned that Catherine is strongly opposed to the interpretation of laws on the basis of court precedents and judicial opinions.[42] Here the Empress departs from her English model and finds herself at one with the juridical thought and practice of central Europe. She also relies on abstract reason rather than on human nature. This she makes clear à propos of torture when she insists on the primacy of reason in reaching judicial decisions or in obtaining a confession or conviction.[43] Strict, reasonable and uniform rules of law are more reliable, permanent, and hence fairer than individuals, however well

---

[36] Notes, f. 164.

[37] But she definitely gives preference to social utility over absolute property rights of individuals. For example, her treatment of the case adduced by Blackstone (*Commentaires*, iv, 355–6) on the duplication of a ferry across the river if it violates the private interest of the first ferry-owner or franchise (Notes, f. 172).

[38] Notes, ff. 60ᵛ, 221 (with special allowance for those on state service).

[39] Ibid. ff. 115ᵛ, 188ᵛ.

[40] Ibid. f. 8.   [41] Ibid. f. 216.   [42] Ibid. f. 116ᵛ.   [43] Ibid. f. 307.

motivated and worthy they might be. We can hear the echo of the perennial cry of Russian reformers: rule by institutions and laws, not by men—although it sounds paradoxical coming from a monarch so strongly committed to the principle of autocratic power.

It is in the area of state administration, however, that our sources provide the most interesting, and previously unnoticed, ideas and suggestions. Taken together they offer the foundation for a new approach to the political organization of the Russian empire. They also show that even in the second half of Catherine's reign, which is often presented as a period of retrenchment and conservatism, the Empress continued to be interested in basic structural change pointing towards the nineteenth century rather than in merely renovating an old machine.

Naturally enough, Catherine upholds clearly and steadfastly the autocratic nature of sovereign power in Russia.[44] At the apex of the state hierarchy stands the sovereign autocratic emperor of all the Russias.[45] He and he alone is the single source of all sovereignty, and therefore of all creative legislation.[46] In her summaries and excerpts from Blackstone she consistently translates or rephrases 'sovereign power' by 'imperial majesty' and 'imperial majesty's power'. She is therefore not very interested in what Blackstone has to say about the nature of English kingship, of the role and relationship of the king to Parliament, etc. These sections of the *Commentaries* are either omitted altogether or summarized briefly, superficially, and not always very accurately.[47] The autocrat's sovereign power is indivisible and inalienable.[48] Officials and institutions have only advisory power and their opinions are never binding on the ruler. In spite of this peremptory assertion of the inviolable character of autocracy, Catherine offers certain ideas and suggestions which to some extent qualify or subtly change its nature.

In the first place, though it is of little but historical significance and simply echoes the Bill of Exclusion, it is emphasized that a ruler of Russia must be of the Greek Orthodox faith.[49] And if the consort of a reigning empress is non-Orthodox or a foreigner, he has no say in the government and no military commitment may be undertaken to defend his foreign interests.[50] In the second place, foreshadowing the legislation

[44] Notes, ff. 10, 13ᵛ.

[45] 'La Majesté Impériale est une personne seule, dont la volonté est uniforme et ferme et dont la personne n'a point d'égale dans l'Empire de Russie, Elle est Supérieure en dignité et en pouvoir à tout autre et jouit d'une existence séparée, toujours capable d'agir dans tous les temps et en tout lieu' (Notes, f. 10ᵛ). Cf. also ibid. f. 14ᵛ.

[46] Notes, f. 16–16ᵛ and f. 183 for personal responsibility to redress wrongs.

[47] Catherine omits the end of Book I, ch. vii and viii ('Of the King's Prerogatives', 'Of the King's Revenue').

[48] Notes, f. 12.

[49] Ibid. Cf. the influence of the Bill of Exclusion in Blackstone, *Commentaires*, i, 302.

[50] Ibid. ff. 6ᵛ and 14ᵛ.

of Paul I which finally resolved (at least in principle) the question of succession left open since the time of Peter the Great, the line of succession is established to and through the first-born male, to his descendants, and then to collateral lines, preference being given to male issue over female.[51] In the third place, if the heir is a minor or mentally or physically handicapped, a regency is instituted under a 'successor' (*preemnik*) or regent (*pravitel'*).[52] The regent would presumably be a close relative of the heir, but his appointment is to be ratified by the Senate and an assembly (sometimes called the 'Chief Executive Chamber') consisting of elected delegates from each province, one for each of the three estates of the realm: nobility, townspeople, and peasants (*sel'skie zhiteli*).[53] Passing reference is made to the power of this assembly to elect or nominate a ruler or regent in the case of the total extinction of the reigning dynasty, but the matter is not further explored. It is, however, stated that the provincial delegates should be present at every coronation.[54] The regent or 'successor' cannot act on the most important matters without consulting the Senate and possibly the Chief Executive Chamber. Upon the ruler's reaching majority, the regent retires to membership of the Imperial Council.[55]

Further provisions are also made for the status of the spouse of the reigning ruler and of the dowager empress.[56] These provisions are of little interest, they are copied from Blackstone's discussion of similar matters in English practice, and they were to receive legislative sanction along similar lines in Paul I's Statute on the Imperial Family (1797). Historically and psychologically it is interesting to note that Catherine's plans were drawn up in direct response to the case of Peter III and were designed to preclude any repetition of her own seizure of power. In other words, the possibility of another Peter III would be ruled out, but so also would a *coup* such as Catherine's of 28 June 1762, which would be completely illegal.

. With respect to the empire Catherine merely restates and stresses the inalienability of its territory and the preclusion of the creation of appanages for any member of the imperial family. For administrative purposes the empire is divided into uniform provinces grouped by regions.[57] The overall scheme also establishes a pyramid of central and subordinate local institutions in a uniform and logical order.[58] The whole territory of the empire is treated alike, though at one point Catherine does state that provinces possessing any special privileges

---

[51] Ibid. 44ᵛ.   [52] Ibid. ff. 11–12.   [53] Ibid. ff. 9ᵛ, 14.

[54] 'Les provinces réunies seront representées à chaque couronnement du souverain par leurs députés savoir trois de chaque gouvernement, un de la Noblesse un des Villes un des Communes' (ibid. f. 6).

[55] Ibid. f. 14–14ᵛ.   [56] Ibid. f. 12–12ᵛ.   [57] Ibid. f. 6–6ᵛ.

[58] Scheme in Notes, f. 18ᵛ—but it may perhaps be a summary of the institutions established in 1775 (the scheme is reproduced in Kologrivov's note referred to in Appendix A).

would be confirmed in them.[59] A significant feature is the provision that each emperor, upon accession, should take an oath to maintain the inalienability of the empire as well as to respect the order of succession.[60] This in itself might lead to a restriction of the autocratic character of supreme power in Russia.

For the higher institutions of the administration Catherine II has nothing of interest and significance to propose. It is noteworthy, though, that she emphasizes the advisory role of the Senate—divided into departments—and of the first three or four colleges (which are also subdivided into departments).[61] In addition, following the description given by Blackstone of the Privy Council, she envisages an imperial council of advisers, selected by the ruler from holders of the three highest service ranks and including the heads of the principal colleges.[62] The council's function and place in the political hierarchy are not specified —probably intentionally, since its main task is to advise on whatever the ruler submits to its consideration. Inasmuch as the Imperial Council had not yet received permanent status and organization, Catherine's notes foreshadow the institution of the *Nepremennyi sovet* in the last years of her reign and its further evolution in the early nineteenth century into its final form as the Council of State in 1810. We might also note that the Council, in a manner not clearly indicated, participates with the Senate in the legislative process. All major acts have to be submitted to the Council for consideration, so that it can give its opinion and advise on the final version.

The most interesting and potentially most significant institutional innovation, which Catherine considered over a long time and in several forms, was the Chief Executive Chamber (*Glavnaya raspravnaya palata*), mentioned earlier in connection with the imperial succession.[63] The idea of a Chief Executive Chamber is put forward quite early in the notes while reading Blackstone. From the context in which it appears, though it is not closely connected with the notes on the *Commentaries*, the idea of a Chief Executive Chamber may have been suggested by Blackstone's discussion of the character and role of Parliament. The first description Catherine gives of the Chief Executive Chamber is, however, quite elaborate, so that it seems probable that she had given it some previous thought. The frequency with which allusions and descriptions of the Chamber appear in the notes on Blackstone, as well as the prominence given to the institution (with modified function, as we shall see)

---

[59] Notes, ff. 6 and 289ᵛ (the latter guarantees freedom of worship to all recognized creeds).

[60] 'Chaque successeur est prié de confirmer et ratifier cet Acte de sa signature et d'y apposer son sceau' (Notes, f. 6ᵛ).

[61] Ibid. ff. 12ᵛ, 14, 17.   [62] Ibid. ff. 12ᵛ–13.

[63] Our analysis and discussion of this proposed institution is based primarily on Catherine's Notes, but in some instances we shall draw on the Drafts as well, for they help to clarify the Empress's intentions. For the question of dating, see the Appendices.

in the drafts on codification, are telling evidence of its central position in the thinking and planning of the Empress.

The Chief Executive Chamber is to consist of three departments:[64] the first with legislative functions which will be discussed below; the second concerned with criminal justice; and the third acting as a high court of equity. In one version there is an incomplete description of a fourth department, the function of which appears to have been to give opinions on the general utility (in economic terms?) of proposed legislation.[65] Leaving aside this fourth department, the character and function of which were not elaborated, we have two judicial boards or courts with review functions in matters criminal and civil, plus the first department. The latter affords a particularly interesting and important insight into Catherine's thinking and the tendency of her ideas on the structural reform of the central government. Except for brief references to the second and third departments (the criminal bench and high court of equity, which obviously parallel the King's Bench and Equity Courts), our description and analysis will concentrate on the first department which, in the Empress's mind, *was* the Chief Executive Chamber.

The most striking feature of the institution planned by Catherine is its membership. Each of the departments would consist of a president (appointed from among the officials in the top three ranks of the official hierarchy), a small number of councillors, and a varying number of assessors. These assessors—or full members in the case of the first department—would be drawn from a body of representatives elected by each *guberniya*. Each of the *gubernii* would have three delegates, one for the nobility, one for the townspeople, and one for the rural estate (i.e. the state peasants).[66] Nowhere is the method of election described, but elections would take place every three years. Ten *guberniya* representatives from each estate are assigned as assessors to each of the two judicial departments; in every case under adjudication the members of the criminal bench or the high court of equity are to be joined by elected representatives from the estate to which the defendants and/or plaintiffs belong. In addition, according to one version of the plan for the Chief Executive Chamber, a representative from the university (i.e. of Moscow) is appointed to sit in the fourth department.[67] Finally, a special school is to be attached to the Chamber, the students of which will receive practical training in administrative and judicial matters.[68] They are presumably to be drawn from university students or young noblemen preparing for a career in the civil service.

[64] The fullest description is given in Notes, f. 9–9^v and Drafts, f. 200.
[65] Drafts, f. 200^v.
[66] Notes, ff. 6^v, 9, and Drafts, f. 200–200^v.
[67] Drafts, f. 205.
[68] Ibid. f. 381.

What were the functions envisaged for this novel institution with representation from the *pays légal* of the provinces? It is always to be remembered that in Catherine's scheme the Chief Executive Chamber —including its first department—is subordinate to the Senate, which stands directly under the autocrat at the top of the governmental pyramid. At times Catherine put the Chamber on the same level as the first three colleges, at others above them, but at no time was it to preempt any function of the Senate. It shares, however, one role with the Senate, namely that of local inspection. In some of the later versions of her plan for the Chief Executive Chamber Catherine proposes regular inspections of the provinces to be carried out by a joint inspectorate drawn from the Senate and the Chamber.[69] Representatives of the latter would have the specific obligation of reviewing the local judiciary, with power to settle pending cases and to clear the courts' dockets, subject to appeal by the parties concerned to the first department of the Chief Executive Chamber in full session and ultimately to the Senate. It would thus appear that the main task of the representatives of the Chamber would be to supervise the proper administration of justice, rather than to make decisions on specific issues of law.

In her notes on Blackstone Catherine gives the first department of the Chief Executive Chamber extensive and important legislative functions. Important and far-reaching legislative acts may be initiated in the Chamber and all such acts are anyway presented for its consideration.[70] The results of its discussions, and the decision reached by the Chief Executive Chamber, are passed on to the Senate for further discussion and thence to the ruler for approval. In case of disagreement with the Senate, the legislation is returned to the Chamber for further consideration; its final conclusions, together with the minutes of the discussion, are then submitted to the sovereign for his decision.[71] A major task of the Chief Executive Chamber is to ensure that new legislation is consonant with existing law and does not infringe the basic laws of the Russian empire.[72] But Catherine makes it quite clear that the Chief Executive Chamber has no independent legislative power, for the sole source of legislation in the empire is the sovereign, and he alone.[73] Yet there is no doubt that, if introduced, the Chief Executive Chamber with its consultative legislative role (one is reminded of the *droits de remonstrance et d'enregistrement* of the French *parlements*) would have been a potentially significant innovation.

At some point, too, Catherine conceived of a supervisory or control-

[69] Drafts, f. 512. The joint team consists of three branches (*kolena*): 1. 'Law and order'. 2. 'Listens and investigates'. 3. 'Accuses and exonerates'. See also ibid. ff. 446ᵛ and 449.

[70] Notes, ff. 6ᵛ, 9.

[71] Drafts, ff. 200ᵛ–201.

[72] Notes, f. 5; for civil cases, Drafts, f. 470.

[73] Notes, f. 5ᵛ.

ling role for the Chief Executive Chamber. Complaints can be addressed
to it and it can sit in judgement on high officials—e.g. governors (*guber-
natory*)—suspected of misdemeanour by constituting itself into a special
high court.[74] The probity of the members of the Chamber would be
guaranteed, it was believed, by prohibiting anyone who had business
dealings with the state (tax farmers in particular) from sitting in the
Chief Executive Chamber.[75] On the model of the English Parliament,
the Chief Executive Chamber is to have supervision over all corporate
bodies, granting their charters and reviewing and inspecting their
activities.[76] It has responsibility not only for private and semi-adminis-
trative bodies such as the *prikazy obshchestvennogo prizreniya* (boards of
social welfare), but also for public educational establishments—schools,
universities, and academies.[77] Finally, in its judicial capacity, the
Chamber participates in the appointment of procurators and in the
supervision of 'colleges of lawyers' (bar associations).[78] Taken together,
Catherine's remarks on the constitution and functions of the Chief
Executive Chamber scattered through her notes on Blackstone's *Commentaries* suggest that the Empress had in mind the establishment in
Russia of a high administrative, legislative, and judicial institution, a
partly representative body with delegates elected by the different
estates from all the provinces of the empire. Presumably non-Russian
populations would be excluded from representation, particularly in
those areas that had not yet received the uniform provincial organization provided by the act of 1775.

On the face of it, Catherine's notes concerning the Chief Executive
Chamber imply the reshaping of the empire's body politic by the creation of a permanent advisory representative institution. As we have seen,
this institution would also play a role at the accession of a new ruler,
especially in the case of a regency and the extinction of the ruling
dynasty. We have also observed that the coronation oath requested of
the monarch would include the promise to preserve this institution as
one of the legal bases of the empire. But as some of the preceding
references have also indicated, Catherine's drafts for codification preserved in the Central State Archives of Ancient Charters placed chief
emphasis on the judicial functions of the Chief Executive Chamber she
planned to create—functions that were mentioned in her notes on the
Commentaries, but not developed there in any significant detail. From

---

[74] Ibid. f. 9ᵛ; Drafts, f. 383ᵛ, and generally with respect to malfeasance in office, Drafts,
ff. 188–9.

[75] Notes, f. 9ᵛ.

[76] Ibid. f. 29ᵛ and Drafts, f. 382.

[77] Notes, ff. 3ᵛ, 29; Drafts, f. 387ᵛ.

[78] 'NB Collège des jurisconsultes is under the supervision of the Chief Executive Chamber
and may be set up and supervised' (Notes, f. 106ᵛ). See also Drafts, ff. 376ᵛ–377 concerning
students attached to the Chamber as *stryapchie* and *khodatai*, and concerning law schools to be
set up also under the supervision of the Chamber.

what we can infer about the chronology of the two sources the drafts for codification are of later date than the notes on Blackstone. The Empress seems, therefore, to have changed her mind so as to limit the significance and the innovatory, not to say revolutionary, character of the proposed institution.[79] But it still may be fairly argued that had even the more limited form of the Chief Executive Chamber been fully implemented, the Russian empire would have been given a solid *Rechtsstaat* foundation that might have served to promote the gradual and smooth modernization of its society and economy in the nineteenth century.

Catherine had alluded to a primarily judicial role for the Chief Executive Chamber in the notes on the *Commentaries* when she spoke of the president of its first department as the 'guardian of justice'.[80] It was a function that seems to have been suggested to her by the duties of the Chancellor in the English (and perhaps also the French) monarchy as she understood them.[81] In fact, the Guardian of Justice was more like an ombudsman in the later Scandinavian tradition—a role which logically and historically fitted better into the framework of the autocracy. Indeed, the task of the Guardian of Justice (or of the Law) was to receive complaints about miscarriages of justice, to right wrongs, and to extend a helping hand to the victims of maladministration.[82] He was to be but an extension of the ruler himself.[83] The personal aspect of political authority was thus fully preserved, while checking any possible abuse of power by the impersonal bureaucracy.

In addition to its function as ombudsman, the Chief Executive Chamber, especially its first department, was to exercise general supervision of the administration of justice. As we have seen, Catherine—at one with most of the enlightened despots of her day—firmly opposed 'judge-made' law. She wanted no part of the English practice of precedent which would lead to decisions and interpretations of law being made by the courts or by other institutions.[84] She even went as far as to prohibit the publication of court decisions on the ground that such publication would make possible the interpretation of the laws, a function which, in her opinion, belonged only to the sovereign as the sole legislative power.[85] It is, therefore, not surprising that Catherine's

[79] For the question of dating, see Appendix B. A comprehensive description of the new structure envisaged is given in Drafts, f. 172–172^v.

[80] '*Khranitel' prav*' (Notes, f. 29^v).

[81] See Notes, ff. 1, 43^v, for obscure references to 'chancelier'.

[82] Drafts, ff. 188–188^v, 383.

[83] Ibid. f. 175, where he is also referred to as *zakonodavets*.

[84] 'NB To this date I am of the opinion that one should not permit the interpretation of laws and any commentaries on them—except [as performed] by the legislative [i.e. sovereign] power' (Notes, f. 210).

[85] 'Les décisions des tribunaux ne doivent jamais être imprimées. Les décisions [des] Tribunaux imprimées et les commentaires sur les lois étouffent la loi' (Drafts, f. 320).

prime concern was to ensure the smooth operation of the mechanism of judicial administration, since it alone guaranteed a correct application of the existing laws.[86] Here the Chief Executive Chamber had to play an important role, not only by exercising its right of periodic inspection but also by *ad hoc* reviews.[87] Finally, the Chamber could be asked to pass judgement on the correctness of procedures followed in any given case, along the lines of the *Cour de cassation* to be established by Napoleon in post-revolutionary France.[88] Also, as mentioned earlier, the second and third departments of the Chamber could act as the highest courts of appeal in criminal and equity cases. In these instances the regular staff was joined by assessors drawn from the elected representatives of the provinces according to the estate of the parties concerned. As supreme guardian of legality and supervisor of correct judicial procedures, the Chief Executive Chamber might have played a very significant role indeed, since this was the area of greatest administrative inefficiency, corruption, and abuse. But the path traced by Catherine was not followed either by herself or by her successors, although it is true that the transformation of the Senate into a primarily judicial body, supervising the administration of justice and, after 1864, acting as a *Cour de cassation,* may be seen as in line with the functions suggested for the Chief Executive Chamber. It may also be noted that the 'explanatory' (providing *raz"yasneniya*) role played by the cassation department of the Senate in the last decades of the imperial regime was precisely what Catherine had in mind for the Chamber once she had abandoned the idea of a consultative representative assembly for legislation and administration.

At first glance the scheme for a Chief Executive Chamber, whether a legislative or a judicial institution or both, seems such an innovation that one looks for models that might have inspired Catherine—for she was rarely very original. Obviously, she was inspired by English institutions of which she was reading in Blackstone at the time she noted her ideas for social and institutional reorganization. But as our presentation has made clear, in fact the English model was not followed at all closely. As Catherine herself put it in her letters to Grimm, she unravelled the thread in her own fashion. She had no intention of introducing any kind of parliament, judicial independence, or legal interpretation. Yet the fact remains that she did have the idea of a legislative consultation, the role of the King's Bench, and the basic principle of equity courts in mind when she was thinking about the Chief Executive Chamber. What she did not seem to realize quite clearly—perhaps she even hid it from herself—was that the English system rested on a social structure that was quite different from that of Russia. In matters of civil law she could hope that her new codification might initiate a trend that would

[86] Ibid. f. 513.   [87] Ibid. ff. 447ᵛ, 449.   [88] Ibid. ff. 178–9, 486ᵛ.

move Russia in the direction of a British-type society; but this obviously would be a very long process and one may well wonder whether it could ever have come to pass as long as serfdom remained the condition of the greater part of the population.

The Chamber's administrative and legislative roles also give it a family resemblance with the newly established Austrian *Reichsrat* (1760) which, as we know, included a few select representatives of the estates from the major provinces of the Habsburg monarchy. There is no evidence in the sources that Catherine had this model consciously in mind. She no doubt knew about the *Reichsrat*, since she was interested in and well-informed about what was going on in Europe; and she also had direct opportunity of gaining information from Joseph II. Austria was a natural source of inspiration, for its administration had been recently reformed, its laws codified, and it too was a large and multinational empire with a social structure akin to Russia's.

But could there not also be Russian origins for some of the suggestions for a Chief Executive Chamber? We may think of Nikita Panin's proposal for an advisory imperial council which was advanced in 1762 but not implemented.[89] But Panin's proposal could have suggested only minor aspects of the Chamber scheme which differs from it in some fundamental respects. As we look closer at the Chief Executive Chamber, however, some interesting antecedents to its provisions come to mind, though it must be emphasized that we have no documentary proof that Catherine was in fact inspired by them. The similarities— such as they are—are functional rather than structural, which makes these parallels even more interesting. Chronologically, the closest 'model' may be found in the proposals of the upper ranks of officials (*generalitet*) and the nobility at the time of the succession crisis of 1730.[90] The reform of the Senate proposed by the *generalitet* would have turned it into a restricted representative body entrusted with the guardianship and supervision of justice. If given life, this institution would have also transmitted information on local conditions and needs, and advised on new legislation. Even more interesting is the parallel provided by the Chief Executive Chamber as a limited consultative representative body with the old Muscovite *zemskie sobory*, especially in their later form of the second half of the seventeenth century. The *sobory*, too, were convened to give information and to advise on proposed major legislation.

[89] Cf. D. Ransel, 'Nikita Panin's Imperial Council Project and the Struggle of Hierarchy Groups at the Court of Catherine II', *Canadian Slavic Studies*, iv (1970), 443–63, and idem, 'Nikita Panin's Role in Russian Court Politics of the Seventeen Sixties: a Critique of the Gentry Opposition Thesis' (dissertation, Yale University, 1969).

[90] If Prince Dmitry Golitsyn had indeed a constitutional plan of settlement in hand, it too bore some faint resemblance to the Chief Executive Chamber as a legislative advisory council. For an introduction to the problem of the crisis of 1730 (and excerpts of documentation), see M. Raeff, *Plans for Political Reform in Imperial Russia* (Englewood Cliffs, N.J., 1966), especially ch. i and the Bibliography (p. 158).

It is true, of course, that the *sobory* were called irregularly and for special purposes only; also they usually included representation only from those groups of the population that were directly concerned with the particular issue at hand. Naturally, the parallels should not be pushed too far, for in a sense they all stem from one common root: the estate assemblies of medieval and early modern Europe.

Be that as it may, Catherine's suggestions not only had precedents both inside and outside Russia, they also had an 'after life'. We have already mentioned certain similarities of the Chief Executive Chamber to the Council of State as shaped by Speransky. More instructive for the historian concerned with the nature and problems of the imperial system is the striking similarity that the Chief Executive Chamber bears to the reform projects of the second half of the nineteenth century. The main objective of these projects was to adjoin to the highest organ of the imperial administration, the Council of State (which had inherited most of the political function of the old Senate), a body representing the population of the provinces. There were differences in the extent of representation proposed, in the manner of election, and in the weighting in favour of one or another social class, but there was no difference in the basic character of the proposed institution: representatives of the empire's population were to be directly consulted in drafting new legislation and in supervising the execution of existing laws and regulations. Moreover the representatives could convey to the highest organ of government information and expressions of needs without submitting them to the sifting and 'censorship' of the bureaucracy. These representatives were to be elected (or selected) on the basis of a narrow franchise and they were merely to inform and advise without any power to bind the autocratic government. Such proposals were made by Grand Duke Constantine, the Minister of the Interior Valuev, and Loris-Melikov. In its most developed form this approach served as the basis for the so-called Bulygin Duma of 1905.

The perennial revival of proposals for this type of reform illustrates the central government's need to establish better communication with the population at a local level, by-passing some of the barriers thrown up by the bureaucracy, and its determination that such communication should pass through existing social organisms (the estates, the *zemstva*). In addition care was always taken that the full sovereign power and responsibility of the ruler should never be seriously questioned or infringed. It bespeaks the difficulty of governing a huge multinational empire solely on a personal basis as well as the need to secure reliable information outside the regular bureaucratic channels and to control its own officials. In retrospect it may seem that these efforts were doomed to failure from the outset since they neither restricted the autocracy nor provided for an active and genuinely representative assembly. But one may ask whether the failure was foreordained in the eighteenth century. Would not the creation of an open, two-way channel of communication between the autocrat and his free subjects and an organ of effective judicial control have improved the administration and made subsequent developments much easier? With hindsight it may be plausibly maintained that the establishment of the Chief Executive Chamber would have prevented the radical, dramatic, and violent split between the autocracy—i.e. the state—and the best educated and active elements of the ruling class and would thus have forestalled the formation of the intelligentsia as a distinct force. And in the absence of a radically inclined intelligentsia the historical destiny of Russia in the nineteenth century (and beyond?) would certainly have been quite different.

Besides opening such avenues for speculating on possible alternative ways of development for Russia, the sources used for the present study also shed interesting light on Catherine's method of work. As was pointed out at the beginning, the manuscript notes of the Empress testify to her industry and attention to detail, to her great curiosity and her knowledge of both foreign literature and Russian practice. Moreover, she enjoyed this legislative work, as she confessed to Baron Grimm:

... sachez et soyez persuadé aussi que chacun a son lot et que le mien est de devenir législomane: régulièrement tous les ans à certaine saison je sens des redoublements qui vont en augmentant; celle de cette année est plus persévérante que celle d'aucune autre, et Dieu merci nous critiquons et nous en savons en plusieurs occasions plus et autant que Blackstone lui-même.[91]

We have also noted her pragmatic and simplificatory bent of mind as well as her concern to introduce innovations into a well-established framework.[92] Unlike Peter I, she was not prepared to discard an institution or break an existing mould in order to introduce something novel. Even when she decided to innovate she proceeded slowly, with constant reference to and reliance on existing conditions and Russian traditions or precedents. Reading foreign literature and listening to others to obtain information and ideas served also to stimulate her own independent thinking.[93] She was also quite conscious of the peculiar, and what today would be called 'backward', nature of her empire, compared to the more dynamic and progressive states of the west, especially France and England. For this reason she felt it necessary first to bring Russia to the level of the contemporary great powers and only then to advance further.

The models she had before her[94] were those of enlightened despotism,

---

[91] Letter of 15 November 1779, 'Pis'ma Ekateriny II . . .' (n. 1), 159.
[92] Drafts, ff. 316 et seq., 480ᵛ; Notes, f. 159ᵛ.   [93] See n. 13.
[94] The events of 1789 only served to confirm Catherine in her preference for the Ancien Régime and to convince her of the dangers both of revolutionary social changes and of the destruction of the estates and 'pouvoirs constitués'.

i.e. strong centralized states with absolute monarchs ruling over societies organized along estate lines. These estates, with a firm legal and
historical basis, provided the framework for ever more active and dynamic socio-economic developments. As Catherine saw it, the task of her
government was to create the legal, social, and economic framework
in which the individual members of the estates could pursue their most
productive and creative activities. A prime requirement was to give
security of property and person to members of these estates.[95] This
was best achieved by means of good laws, fair and efficient administration of justice, and the establishment of adequate channels of
communication which would enable the autocracy and central
government to redress wrongs immediately and to be accurately
informed of the country's needs and wishes. The serfs were excluded
from this scheme, since they were considered and treated as the
children, the 'wards' of their lords.[96] Seen in this perspective,
Catherine was not so much trying to create the *bürgerliche Gesellschaft*
in Hegel's (and Marx's) nineteenth-century sense, but rather the
polity—civil society—that Frederick II and Kant wrote about.
But in Russia, which did not yet possess the legal and institutional
framework of such a polity, the first task was to create estates, give
them a firm legal foundation, and extend protection and security for
their members' activities in pursuing their lawful economic and
cultural interests. This is what codification was all about, and this is
what Catherine hoped to achieve by setting up the Chief Executive
Chamber.

   If such indeed were her long-term intentions, then taking into consideration her careful pragmatism and socio-political timidity, we
should be less surprised that she accomplished little than that she
accomplished anything at all. When all is said and done, she did leave
Russia with a stronger institutional and legal framework, with a more
rational and better-ordered—and hence more efficient—central administration and, most important perhaps, with the elements of corporate self-government for the upper classes and the idea of directed
social and economic development, a development which would be led
by the most dynamic and successful members of the recognized estates
of the realm.

   The Empress herself had no illusions and possessed too clear a sense
of her political possibilities to see her reign as an unmitigated success
and the crowning achievement of the process of Russia's westernization.

---

[95] Drafts, f. 198ᵛ.

[96] J.-L. Van Regemorter, 'Deux images idéales de la paysannerie russe à la fin du xviiiᵉ s.',
Cahiers du Monde russe et soviétique, ix (1968), 5–19, and M. Confino, 'La politique de tutelle
des seigneurs russes envers leurs paysans vers la fin du xviiiᵉ siècle', *Revue des études slaves*,
xxxvii (1960), 39–69, and idem, 'Le paysan russe jugé par la noblesse au xviiiᵉ siècle', ibid.
xxxviii (1961), 51–63.

Her chastening realism is best expressed in an interesting note she wrote to herself:

Use the winter of 1787 and the beginning of 1788 to compose the chapters on the Senate and the Senate's procedures and instruction, do this with application and honest industry, if however the information [received] and criticism reveal barriers and annoying (*skuchnye*) or cunning (*lukavye*) difficulties, then put the whole work away (*v dolgii yashchik*), for we do not see (?) for whose sake I labour and will not my labours, care and warm concern for the good of the empire be in vain, for I do see that I cannot make my frame of mind (*umopolozhenie*) hereditary.[97]

Did she think only of Grand Duke Paul when she mused on the impossibility of transmitting her attitudes? Or did she also consider the relative backwardness of Russian society for whom many of her plans and expectations might seem premature? We do not know. But what we do know is that this was not just the passing mood of a tired, old, and disenchanted woman. Throughout her life she had displayed a similar attitude and followed this line of conduct, so that her reign—and her legislative activities—constitute an organic unity. It was this unity of outlook and approach that played a major role in setting the course for the subsequent evolution of Russia. Perhaps the best and most accurate epitaph we can write in conclusion is that Catherine's plans, aims, efforts, and partial success created the framework for the transformation of society in the first quarter of the nineteenth century and, at one remove, the *sine qua non* for the reforms of the 1860s. Paradoxically her legislative achievement provided both the foundation for the emergence of modern Russian society and the cause of the empire's institutional rigidity.

APPENDIX A

The manuscript of the notes that Catherine II took while reading a French translation of Blackstone's *Commentaries* consists of 386 folio pages, large format, written on both sides with margins of about half-page width on the left side. The paper is gilt edged, the ink is faded roughly every ten pages for about two to three pages. The manuscript is part of the Panin *fond* preserved in the Manuscript Department of the Lenin State Library in Moscow. There is no indication as to how it came to be among the Panin papers—presumably the copy was given by Catherine to Count Nikita Panin. It is incorrectly dated and catalogued under the general heading 'Materials for the Nakaz to the Commission (1767)' (*Materialy k nakazu Kommissii*). The manuscript bears pencilled markings collating the notes with the French translation of the *Commentaries*. I suspect that these collations (as well as the pagination) were the work of Ya. L. Barskov who worked on the literary and cultural aspects of Catherine's reign after the Revolution. His identifications, notices

[97] Drafts, f. 296 (original punctuation retained).

of use, and explanatory marginalia may be found on other documents of this collection.

The only reference to this manuscript in the published literature known to me is a brief notice by S. N. Kologrivov, 'Novonaidennyi trud Ekateriny Velikoi', *Russkii arkhiv*, 1908, no. 6, pp. 169–77. But Kologrivov refers to a fair copy in a clerk's hand deposited in the archives of the Council of State. From his description I would suspect that Catherine had her notes copied (which may explain why she gave the original to Panin) and it is this second copy that was preserved with her other official papers. But Kologrivov's reliability is in question since he makes the erroneous assertion that there was no contemporary French translation of Blackstone which Catherine could have used and offers the wild hypothesis that she read a privately prepared digest. His notice is of no interest, for it contains only a few random quotations from Catherine's notes which he makes no attempt to analyse or put into context.

The entire document in the Panin *fond* is written in Catherine's hand; for many pages at a time she merely extracts and summarizes, with only occasional 'NBs' in parentheses or a brief phrase or term in Russian inserted in the French text. The summary and excerpts are in French, though the spelling and, on occasion, the grammar are faulty. On the whole, Catherine keeps close to the French text she is reading, but on many pages, especially in the first part of the manuscript, she intersperses the excerpts with her own remarks, suggestions, and proposals. Sometimes it is not altogether clear from her text whether she is describing existing conditions or making proposals for the future. She also quotes Russian equivalents, notes Russian precedents or special circumstances, and makes memoranda for herself. These comments are found either within the text of the excerpts or in the margins—some of these passages bear many corrections with much crossing out and writing over (e.g. the section dealing with the succession to the Russian throne). Almost invariably these comments are written in highly ungrammatical and incorrect Russian (the mistakes reveal a native German speaker), and some sentences are difficult to understand or give rise to possible misinterpretation owing to the hopeless confusion of declensional endings and genders. It should be noted, however, that in spite of Catherine's obvious lack of grammatical proficiency, Russian was the language that came most readily to her when she wanted to state her own ideas.

The text of the *Commentaries* that the Empress read was the first French translation:

Commentaires sur les Loix Angloises de M. Blackstone, Traduits de l'Anglois par M. D. G***. Sur la quatrième Edition d'Oxford. 6 Tomes. A Bruxelles Chez J. L. de Boubers, Imprimeur-Libraire, Marché aux Herbes. M DCC LXXIV—M DCC LXXVI Avec Permission.

A brief comparison of original and translation shows that the translation is very loose: the French text is more wordy, at times goes beyond Blackstone's meaning and contains some fanciful expansions. A detailed comparison between the original, the translation, and the excerpts made by Catherine might yield a suggestive picture of the transmission of ideas and of the shift in tone and connotation that may accompany the process.

Catherine's own comments and notes are more frequent and extensive in the early part of the manuscript. In fact, we find most of the institutional proposals on the first 23 folios. From the last three volumes of the translation Catherine for the most part simply makes excerpts with practically no comment or annotation. It would thus appear that the stimulation provided by the early volumes of the *Commentaries*, which deal with the political and institutional organization of England, declined as time went on. However, Catherine was interested in the civil law expounded in the *Commentaries* and summarized it carefully and at some length.

These observations raise the question of the dating of the manuscript. From her letter to Grimm, cited at the beginning of this study (p. 18), we know that the Empress was reading Blackstone almost as soon as the French translation appeared. In addition, on folio 67 of the manuscript there is a direct reference to the rules of Armed Neutrality for seaborne commerce and maritime law, which would date that particular part as not earlier than 1780. Finally, we also have allusions to the *Politseiskii reglament* of 1782, which extends the period of the reading still further.[98] In the light of this and the observations on the documents discussed in Appendix B, it seems most probable that Catherine read the *Commentaries* (and took notes on them) over a period of several years, *c.* 1774–82. If the notes on the Chief Executive Chamber in the earlier folios also date from the earliest reading period, one may ask whether Catherine did not think of establishing the elected body as part of the provincial reforms and in direct response to the need for better communication and information which the Pugachev revolt had demonstrated. But this is merely a hypothetical question based on the present source. Clearly the notion was not a passing one, as the references to it in the latter part of the manuscript indicate.

APPENDIX B

The source in question is a bound volume deposited in the Central State Archives of Ancient Charters (Tsentral'nyi gosudarstvennyi arkhiv drevnikh aktov: TsGADA) in Moscow, catalogued as No. 17 of Section (*razryad*) x, in the Archives of the Council of State. It is labelled 'Materials for Codification' and consists of several hundred folios of varying origin and form. Most of them are in a copyist's hand, though there are many written by Catherine herself; some of the former contain notes and corrections made in her hand. The text is in Russian throughout; it is grammatically correct, except for Catherine's own annotations. Most of the items, some of which are of substantial length and 'books' in their own right, are without title, although practically all relate to matters of legislation and, especially, codification. There are also several fair copies of excerpts from existing legislation and earlier laws (e.g. inheritance provisions of the *Ulozhenie* of 1649). It is impos-

---

[98] For example, Notes, ff. 39, 65, 107, 122ᵛ, 195ᵛ.

sible to suggest a logical order and dating for this material. Papers found in the imperial cabinet were collected more or less according to subject matter and bound together when sufficient material for a volume had been assembled. There is much repetition and duplication, some drafts having been copied several times, sometimes with minor stylistic changes, perhaps to provide copies for the Empress's advisers.

The connection between this cento of materials and the notes on Blackstone's *Commentaries* is made by Catherine herself. In the codification drafts she frequently notes: 'cf. French notes on Blackstone, page . . .'—and the reference is clearly to the text we have used.[99] These references are scattered throughout the material, so that we may infer that these draft proposals and memoranda were written after her reading of Blackstone. The drafts also illustrate the change in the character and function of the first department of the Chief Executive Chamber which is discussed in the present essay. We have further grounds to date these notes later than Catherine's reading of Blackstone on the basis of specific references made to the *Uprava blagochiniya* of 1782.[100] I did not find in these documents any direct reference to the Charters to the Nobility and to the Towns (1785). This is strange, for the ideas contained in these charters were certainly under discussion for some time before their promulgation. It is true, of course, that the concrete institutional framework for estate self-government had been introduced by the Statute on the Provinces of 1775. That Catherine's small note to herself quoted at the end of this essay and clearly dated late 1787 may be considered as a *terminus ad quem* of the entire material seems highly probable, but not absolutely certain.[101]

[99] For example, Drafts, ff. 201, 461 ('NB About this see folio 122 of French notes from Blackstone and the relevant Russian law'), 464, 480.

[100] Drafts, f. 180 gives a specific date, 26 August 1785, in connection with *zakonodavets* ('Le Chancellier de Justice') and his duties.

[101] The research for this study was carried out during my participation in the academic exchange programme between the Academy of Sciences of the U.S.S.R. and the American Council of Learned Societies administered by the International Research Exchange Board. I should like to thank the officials of these institutions, as well as the staff of the Manuscript Department of the Lenin State Library and of the Central State Archives of Ancient Charters (TsGADA). I am also grateful to the National Endowment for the Humanities and the International Research Exchange Board for financial support.

S. E. Desnitsky, Adam Smith, and the *Nakaz* of Catherine II

By A. H. BROWN

SEMEN EFIMOVICH DESNITSKY has strong claims to be regarded as one of the most outstandingly able Russian social and political thinkers of the second half of the eighteenth century. He was certainly one of the most influential figures in Moscow University circles from the late sixties to the middle eighties of the eighteenth century, and he is regarded both by pre-revolutionary and by Soviet legal historians as 'the father of Russian jurisprudence'.[1]

Desnitsky was also an important link between British and Russian social and legal thought at this time. As the translator of the first volume of Blackstone's *Commentaries* into Russian,[2] he helped to make the English jurist's ideas more widely known in Russia, but he played a role of even greater significance by introducing many of the ideas of Adam Smith and of other Scottish Enlightenment theorists (such as Millar, Robertson, and Kames) into Catherine II's Russia.[3] Though Desnitsky was not, of course, alone among educated Russians in his awareness of the work of Smith, Robertson, and other members of the 'Scottish Historical School', he was the first Russian to take up a number of Smithian ideas. This he was in a peculiarly advantageous position to do since, along with a Russian colleague, Ivan Andreevich Tret'yakov (who, like Desnitsky, was appointed to a chair of law in Moscow in 1768), Desnitsky had been sent to Glasgow University in 1761 where he and Tret'yakov remained until 1767. During the first two and a half years of their studies in Glasgow, Adam Smith was still a professor there, and the Russian students attended his lectures and heard him expound many of the arguments which Smith himself did

---

[1] See, for example, A. V. Evrov, 'Istoriya metod nauki zakonovedeniya v XVIII veke', *Zhurnal Ministerstva narodnogo prosveshcheniya*, 1835 no. 6, vyp. 2; *Biograficheskii slovar' professorov i prepodavatelei Imperatorskogo Moskovskogo universiteta*, i (M., 1855), 297; I. S. Bak, *Istoriya russkoi ekonomicheskoi mysli* (ed. A. I. Pashkov), i (M., 1955), especially 571; and S. A. Pokrovsky, *Politicheskie i pravovye vzglyady S. E. Desnitskogo* (M., 1955).

[2] Only Volume i of Blackstone's *Commentaries on the Laws of England* was translated by Desnitsky. It appeared in three parts under the title *Istolkovaniya anglinskikh zakonov g. Blakstona* (Moscow University Press; I, 1780; II, 1781; III, 1782). The translation is of a very high quality, though occasionally it contains slight and apparently deliberate deviations from Blackstone's text. It also includes many annotations by Desnitsky, a number of which express his disagreement with particular views of Blackstone and some of which reflect the alternative views of Adam Smith and of John Millar.

[3] See A. H. Brown, 'Adam Smith's First Russian Followers' in: A. Skinner and T. Wilson (eds.), *Adam Smith: Bicentenary Essays* (Oxford) (forthcoming).

not commit to print until 1776 with the publication of *The Wealth of Nations*.[4] They also studied under the supervision of one of Smith's most brilliant pupils, John Millar, another pioneer in the social sciences, who held the chair of law in Glasgow from 1761 until his death in 1801.

The influence of Smith and Millar on Desnitsky's thought may be detected in virtually every published work of the Russian jurist. They were not, of course, the only influences on Desnitsky's intellectual development. Though Desnitsky was critical of Blackstone in certain respects, he also accepted a number of Blackstone's ideas, and the influence of Lomonosov may also be detected in his work. But the central features of Desnitsky's approach to the study of law and society —his comparative-historical method and the stadial theory of development which he employed—were direct fruits of his period of study in Scotland.

Desnitsky rejects the idea that 'the various successes of the human race, its risings and falling' can be measured 'on the basis of its imputed childhood, youth, maturity, and old age' and observes that 'fortunately for our times, the newest and most assiduous explorers of human nature have discovered incomparably better means for studying nations in their various successes in accordance with the circumstances and conditions through which those peoples, starting from their primordial society with wild animals, rose to the highest degree of greatness and enlightenment'.[5] Desnitsky goes on to outline 'four such conditions of the human race' (conditions which, he suggests, were recognized also by ancient writers) of which the most primitive is 'the *condition* of peoples living by *hunting* animals and feeding on the *spontaneous fruits* of the earth; the second is the *condition* of people living as shepherds, or the *pastoral*; the third is the *agricultural*; the fourth and last is the *commercial*'.[6] These stages of development are precisely those which were recognized by

[4] See the characteristically judicious essay of Academician M. P. Alekseev, 'Adam Smith and his Russian Admirers of the Eighteenth Century', Appendix VII of W. R. Scott's *Adam Smith as Student and Professor* (Glasgow, 1937), 424–31. See also G. Sacke, 'Die Moskauer Nachschrift der Vorlesungen von Adam Smith', *Zeitschrift für Nationalökonomie* (Vienna), Bd. ix (3), 351–6; and N. W. Taylor, 'Adam Smith's First Russian Disciple' in *The Slavonic and East European Review*, xlv (1967), 425–38. Taylor's article is devoted to I. A. Tret'yakov, a scholar who, strictly speaking, should not be given precedence over Desnitsky as a transmitter of Adam Smith's ideas. While it should be emphasized that Desnitsky (unlike Tret'yakov) also did very much more than this, he did introduce many of Smith's ideas (sometimes in the form of verbatim renderings of passages in Smith's lectures) as early as 1768 in his *Slovo o pryamom i blizhaishem sposobe k naucheniyu yurisprudentsii*. The only work published as early as 1768 which bears Tret'yakov's name is the *Slovo o proisshestvii i uchrezhdenii universitetov v Evrope na gosudarstvennykh izhdiveniyakh*. But this work, as I pointed out in my article, 'S. E. Desnitsky i I. A. Tret'yakov v Glazgovskom universitete (1761–1767)' (*Vestnik Moskovskogo universiteta: Istoriya*, 1969 no. 4, pp. 75–88) was in fact composed by Desnitsky.

[5] S. E. Desnitsky, *Yuridicheskoe rassuzhdenie o raznykh ponyatiyakh, kakie imeyut narody o sobstvennosti imeniya v razlichnykh sostoyaniyakh obshchezhitel'stva* (Moscow University Press, 1781). It is reprinted in full in S. A. Pokrovsky (ed.), *Yuridicheskie proizvedeniya progressivnykh russkikh myslitelei: vtoraya polovina XVIII veka* (M., 1959), 242–58. The passage quoted above appears on p. 244. [6] *Ibid.*

Adam Smith and John Millar and employed by them as tools of analysis in their Glasgow lectures.[7] However, they figure, if anything, even more prominently in Desnitsky's public lectures, and in none more so than his *Yuridicheskoe rassuzhdenie o nachale i proiskhozhdenii supruzhestva u pervonachal'nykh narodov i o sovershenstve, k kakomu onoe privedennym byt' kazhetsya posledovavshimi narodami prosveshchenneishimi* (1775) (a work which owes a lot to Millar)[8] and his *Yuridicheskoe rassuzhdenie o raznykh ponyatiyakh, kakie imeyut narody o sobstvennosti imeniya v razlichnykh sostoyaniyakh obshchezhitel'stva* (1781) (an exceptionally systematic discussion of the four-stage theory of development).

In almost all of his works, Desnitsky emerges as a proponent of legal and political reform as well as a social theorist. The range of his writings includes, however, those in which he is mainly concerned with sociological analysis of a broad, generalizing type and others in which his main concern is with practical proposals for political reform. It is Desnitsky's most important work in the latter category, his *Predstavlenie o uchrezhdenii zakonodatel'noi, suditel'noi i nakazatel'noi vlasti v Rossiiskoi imperii*, with which I shall be concerned in this article, and I wish to pay particular attention to the last of four appendices which Desnitsky added to this work, that devoted to state finances.

Some attention must, first of all, however, be devoted to the *Predstavlenie* as a whole. Desnitsky wrote this remarkable work in response to the setting-up of Catherine II's Legislative Commission in 1767 and completed it early in 1768. Since it was addressed to Catherine herself, it was not published during Desnitsky's lifetime and, in fact, it remained unknown to scholars until 1905, the date of its first publication.[9] Yet

[7] See Brown, op. cit. (n. 3), and R. L. Meek, 'Smith, Turgot, and the "Four Stages" Theory', *The History of Political Economy*, iii (1971), 9–27.

[8] Cf. John Millar, *Observations Concerning the Distinction of Ranks in Society* (1771), especially the first two chapters. Desnitsky's explanation of the improvement of the position of women in society in terms of their increasing usefulness in the domestic economy takes up a major theme of Millar's. A great number of Desnitsky's particular examples and detailed citations may also be found in Millar. Desnitsky never refers to this book by Millar and the fact that it was not published until four years after his return to Russia may well mean that he never saw it. It is highly probable that it was the lectures of Millar which Desnitsky attended that were the major influence here rather than Millar's book, for Desnitsky was not slow to refer to books by other leading figures of the Scottish Enlightenment (such as Hume, Kames, and Robertson) and in particular to Smith's *Theory of Moral Sentiments*. We know from a letter in Glasgow University archives written by Desnitsky on 31 December 1765 that he had been attending Millar's classes ever since 1762 and other archival evidence in Glasgow shows that throughout 1766 and until his departure from Scotland in 1767 he continued to work more closely with Millar than with any other Glasgow professor.

[9] Desnitsky's *Predstavlenie* was first published under the editorship of A. I. Uspensky in *Zapiski Imperatorskoi Akademii nauk*, vii, no. 4 (1905). It has been reprinted twice. The first occasion was in a collection of works by Desnitsky and others edited by I. Ya. Shchipanov, *Izbrannye proizvedeniya russkikh myslitelei vtoroi poloviny XVIII veka*, i (1952), 292–332; the second in Pokrovsky, op. cit. (n. 5), 101–42. The 1952 edition lacks Desnitsky's second appendix to his text (on church government), but the Pokrovsky reprint is complete. All subsequent citations of the *Predstavlenie* are from this latter collection.

the *Predstavlenie* has strong claims to be regarded as Desnitsky's most interesting single work and it is one which shows him to be an astute and independent political thinker. In it, Desnitsky elaborates a detailed plan of political reform for Russia, applying in an original way ideas about government which he had learned from observation, as well as from books and lectures, during the six years he spent in Britain. Though the British constitutional model was clearly one which Desnitsky found attractive, his proposals do not follow it in all respects but, on the contrary, are carefully adapted to Russian conditions.

Desnitsky not only discusses the setting-up of legislative, judicial, and executive authorities in the Russian empire, as the title of his work suggests, but he also introduces a fourth section to the main body of proposals entitled *grazhdanskaya vlast'*, in which he makes detailed proposals for the reform of local government, and he concludes his work with appendices on state inhabitants 'of lower birth', on church government, on the Cossacks and nomadic peoples in the Russian empire, and on state financial policy and organization. In order to devote adequate space to a discussion of the last of these appendices, only brief notice can be taken of some of the most salient points in each of the four sections of the main body of Desnitsky's text.

In his first section on the legislative authority, Desnitsky proposes a radical reform of the senate whereby it would become an elected body composed of some six to eight hundred persons. It was to be composed not only of landowners in the various regions and provinces but of merchants and handicraftsmen, as well as ecclesiastics and scholars. Landowners were to be elected by their fellow landowners and the senators drawn from trade and commerce were to be elected by the merchants and craftsmen themselves, subject to a property qualification. Bishops with a diocese entrusted to them were to be allowed to become senators without election, whereas universities and other educational institutions, such as colleges of sciences and of arts, were to elect from their midst whomsoever they thought fit, 'persons able to live on their own means, and who will make representations on their behalf'.[10] Desnitsky finds it expedient to stress, however, that 'in Russia . . . the monarchical condition and the unity of the fatherland' demand that this senate would have less independence than the parliaments of Britain and France and that its relationship to the monarch would be essentially an advisory one.[11]

In his proposals for the establishment of the judicial authority, Desnitsky suggests that there should be at least eight judicial circuits established in the Russian empire and centred upon such places as Riga, St. Petersburg, Tobol'sk, Novgorod, Moscow, and Kazan'. In each of these regions the judicial authority would be composed of twelve people

---

[10] *Predstavlenie*, 104.   [11] Ibid. 105.

comprising an advocate-general, four judges of criminal cases, and seven general judges of both civil and criminal affairs.[12] Desnitsky also advocates trial by jury. He expresses the hope that Russian monarchs might be 'graciously inclined to legislate according to English example and to legalize the selection from among forty outsiders fifteen witnesses' who would be chosen from among the inhabitants of the town in which the court was sitting for the duration of the trial. Having heard the entire case, it would be the duty of these jurors to say under oath whether the accused was guilty or not and that having been done, it would be 'the business of the judge to pronounce judgement in accordance with their vote or in accordance with the majority of their votes, and to order that this judgement should be executed'.[13]

In fact there is rather more of a Scots example than of an 'English example', to be detected in Desnitsky's proposals for a jury system. In England at that time twelve jurymen were chosen from a group of forty and they were required to reach a unanimous decision. (It was not until the passing of the Criminal Justice Act of 1967 that the possibility of a majority verdict was introduced into English law.) In Scotland, however, the number of jurors was fifteen (as in Desnitsky's proposal) and they were permitted to reach a majority verdict.

Adam Smith, in a course of lectures attended by Desnitsky in 1762–3, drew attention to this very point. Referring to the English jury system, he said: 'The chief defect is that this jury must be unanimous in their opinion, unless they would choose to be greatly harassed and threatened with ignominy. And in this our Scots juries, though they do not appear to be so well contrived in other points, appear to be superior, as they are not required to be unanimous. It is very hard that they should thus be obliged to declare themselves of one opinion. The best men, and of the greatest integrity, may differ, and each think himself altogether certain that the matter is so; this must arise from the variety of human tempers, and the different lights in which men see things. . . .' Smith went on to emphasize that matters in Scotland were 'on a very different footing. The number which is required to a jury is fifteen. Nor is unanimity required of these. It was some time ago, but has within the last 150 years gone into desuetude. . . .'[14]

British experience, and possibly the direct influence of Smith, has also some bearing on Desnitsky's emphasis on the importance of judges

---

[12] *Predstavlenie*, 107.

[13] Ibid. 109.

[14] The quotations are from a manuscript report of Smith's 'Lectures on Jurisprudence', taken by a fellow student of Desnitsky in Glasgow in 1762–3 (Glasgow University Library: MS. Gen. 94, vol. 5, pp. 38 and 40). The manuscript is to be published by the Clarendon Press under the editorship of R. L. Meek, D. D. Raphael, and P. G. Stein. The same comparison between English and Scots law on juries is to be found in an abbreviated form in the set of student notes of Smith's lectures published under the editorship of Edwin Cannan. See Adam Smith, *Lectures on Justice, Police, Revenue and Arms* (Oxford, 1896), 52–3.

holding office for life, a point which is likewise stressed in Smith's lectures referred to above. The necessity of a judge remaining in office until his death arises, Desnitsky argues, from the need to safeguard him from threats to his independence and the necessity of enabling him 'to judge everyone without exception'. Desnitsky argues for the establishment of advocates in view of the fact that 'in many states it has been found by experience that in the absence of argument in court there is no other means of achieving justice'.[15] He supports the restoration of capital punishment for the crime of murder and does so by employing the specifically Smithian *terminology* (and, in an incomplete form, Smith's *concept*) of the 'impartial spectator'.[16]

So far as the executive power is concerned, Desnitsky suggests that this may be safely entrusted to governors in the provinces and in the best-known provincial towns only, so that one governor will not be dependent upon another but all will be directly responsible to the monarch. Such a decree he holds to be necessary in order to prevent great personages from overthrowing the governor because of the strictness which he would exercise in the fulfilment of his duties. Not only the governor, however, must be safeguarded from arbitrary interference. So must the people of the province be given protection against arbitrary action on the part of the governor himself. To ensure that he does not harm the innocent, he should be held answerable to the twelve judges in the chief provincial courts who 'must at every trial publicly ask those present whether there are any complaints against the governor and whether anyone has suffered any harm from him'.[17] Should a complaint or instance of injury turn up, the judges must report this to the senate, 'where the governor will be subjected to a fine and punishment at the monarch's pleasure'.[18]

The main duties of the governor would be to maintain peace and order within the area of his jurisdiction, to arrest criminals, and to keep those convicted in prison. For these purposes he would have under his control soldiers to assist him—one hundred infantrymen and twenty cavalrymen for the ordinary provincial governor and two thousand eight hundred in the capital cities. The governor is also entrusted with the duty of gathering such poll-taxes and duties from landed property owners within his province as will be decreed by the senate.[19]

In the fourth part of the main body of Desnitsky's proposals, that devoted to the civic authority, there is ample demonstration of Desnitsky's belief that the 'commercial' stage of development is the highest stage to which society can advance and of his desire to further

[15] *Predstavlenie*, 110.
[16] Ibid. 113. Cf. Adam Smith, *Theory of Moral Sentiments* (1759). See also D. D. Raphael, 'The Impartial Spectator' (Dawes Hicks Lecture on Philosophy), *The Proceedings of the British Academy*, lviii (1972), 1–22.
[17] *Predstavlenie*, 114.   [18] Ibid.   [19] Ibid.

the interests of merchants and craftsmen and reduce the powers of the nobility. He stresses that civic power must be in the hands of those who live in the towns and, in particular, of the merchants and craftsmen. He proposes a civic authority of seventy-three people in the capital . cities consisting of eighteen noblemen living in the city and fifty-five merchants.[20] For the principal provincial towns he proposes a smaller civic authority, but one in which merchants would also be in a clear majority.[21]

In the capital cities the civic authority of Desnitsky's design would be divided into six departments, each consisting of twelve people, while one member out of the seventy-three would be elected by his colleagues to be president of this local authority. Desnitsky's plan envisages a high degree of civic planning and supervision. The functions which he allots to the second department are of special interest as a clear instance of Desnitsky *rejecting* one of Adam Smith's major tenets. To the second department Desnitsky allocates the task of keeping an eye on 'the cheapness of foodstuffs to be sold in the particular city . . . that is, to observe a zealous supervision so that in all shops and in all markets the goods are sold at a known price and by weight and measure established by state decree. And in addition to that, the duty of the second department will be to stamp out profiteers and middlemen who, by increasing the price of things, cause the inhabitants unnecessary loss and make it difficult for them to maintain themselves.'[22] While Adam Smith was well aware of the danger of traders acting in consort to raise prices, he believed that to provide other traders with access to the market would be a more effective means of keeping prices down than price regulation by any local or national authority.[23]

The duty of Desnitsky's first department is to conduct the affairs of the town in such a manner as their loan regulations will allow or the law of the senate require. The third department is charged with the supervision of the civic architecture, so that building will take place according to a plan prescribed by the senate and the town will not suffer from overcrowding or incongruities arising out of disorderly building or from buildings which are falling apart. The fourth department has the task of supervision of the repair of streets and canals, the removal of refuse, and the provision of street lighting. The task of the fifth is to collect duties from the inhabitants and traders in accordance with local needs while keeping within the limits laid down for the civic authority by the senate. The sixth department is charged with settling petty civil disputes where no criminal action is involved, such as the differences which will arise between cabmen, inn-keepers, and itinerant traders.[24]

[20] *Predstavlenie*, 117.   [21] Ibid. 119.   [22] Ibid. 118.
[23] Cf. Adam Smith, *The Wealth of Nations* (ed. E. Cannan), (University Paperback edition, 1961), i, especially 144 and 159.   [24] *Predstavlenie*, 118.

The *Predstavlenie* as a whole contains many more acute observations and interesting proposals for reform than can be discussed within the scope of the present article. In summary, it is fair to say that its implementation would have set Russia far along the path towards constitutional monarchy. Desnitsky is an opponent of arbitrary power in all its forms, whether that of a provincial governor, of a landowner, or (though here he has to be more guarded) of an autocrat. Though it goes without saying that he cannot attack the absolute power of the monarch directly, Desnitsky's desire to create strong political institutions and his advocacy of a separation of the legislative, judicial, executive, and civic authorities, so that one would act as an overseer and check upon another, would lead not only to a curb upon the power of the nobility and (especially given the social composition proposed by Desnitsky for the legislature and the civic authorities) an increase in the power of commercial and professional interests. It would also have its effect upon the autocracy. The establishment of a representative assembly, of an independent judiciary, and of an executive authority subordinate to the law could scarcely, except in the very short term, be compatible with a continuation of the absolute power of the monarch. Given Desnitsky's close familiarity with, and admiration for, the British constitutional model, it is more than likely that he anticipated just such a gradual development towards constitutional monarchy.

It is highly probable that Catherine read the whole of Desnitsky's *Predstavlenie* and certain that she read at least part of it. It is an interesting but little-known fact that many points from Desnitsky's fourth appendix to his *Predstavlenie* (*O uzakonenii finanskom*) are incorporated by Catherine in the Second Supplement to her *Nakaz* which she completed on 8 April 1768. Since there are a number of clear traces of Adam Smith's influence on this fourth appendix of Desnitsky, it is evident that not only Desnitsky but (indirectly) Adam Smith exercised influence over Catherine's famous *Nakaz* which was published in Russian, French, German, and English eight years before the publication of *The Wealth of Nations* (in which Smith, *inter alia*, developed a number of the points that, via his Glasgow lectures, had appeared in the *Nakaz*). Some of Desnitsky's observations are taken over word for word by Catherine; others are somewhat altered; and some, of course, are ignored. But a sufficient number of entire sentences from the *Predstavlenie* are adopted by Catherine to put her debt to him beyond doubt.

In principle, Desnitsky's priority with regard to the material used in the *Nakaz* could be challenged. The main body of Desnitsky's *Predstavlenie* is dated 30 February 1768, an obvious mistake, though one which nevertheless suggests that the work was submitted for the attention of the monarch and her legislative commission at the end of February or beginning of March of that year. (Desnitsky, like Adam Smith, appears to have suffered from absent-mindedness.[25] Apart from this slip over dates, an example is also to be found in the letter which he wrote hurriedly on 31 December 1765, for submission to a Glasgow University Faculty meeting the same day. At the end of the letter, written in English, he inserts the Russian word *goda* after the date.)

The circumstances of the discovery of the *Predstavlenie o uchrezhdenii zakonodatel'noi, suditel'noi i nakazatel'noi vlasti v Rossiiskoi imperii* are described by Aleksandr Uspensky in his introduction to the publication in *Zapiski Imperatorskoi Akademii nauk*.[26] The main part of Desnitsky's work was contained in a notebook of English paper, consisting of twenty-five unnumbered pages of small writing. Beside it in the archive in which it was discovered were four other notebooks (also of English paper) in which further (and even more detailed) advice to Catherine's legislative commission is to be found. There is no doubt that Uspensky was right in his judgement that both circumstantial evidence and the internal evidence of the texts indicate that these further proposals are also Desnitsky's work. Conceivably it could be argued that they were written later than the main part of the text and that Desnitsky incorporated entire sentences from Catherine's Second Supplement to the *Nakaz* rather than the other way round. This, however, is an exceedingly unconvincing explanation of the correspondence between the texts. Desnitsky's writings invariably begin and end with the conventional, and virtually obligatory, tributes to the great wisdom and talents of the Empress, and the main text of his *Predstavlenie* is no exception to this general rule. It is unthinkable that in an appendix to that text, he could quote sentence after sentence from a newly-published work by Catherine without acknowledgement of, or tribute to, his source. For Catherine, on the other hand, nothing could have been simpler than the incorporation in her own work, without acknowledgement, of points made by a still obscure scholar, especially since she did not trouble to acknowledge many of her borrowings in the *Nakaz* from the most illustrious European thinkers of her time.[27]

[25] As Ramsay of Ochertyre noted, Smith 'sometimes offended serious people by laughing or smiling in the time of divine worship. They did not know that he was so much absorbed in thought, that he knew nothing of what was going on' (*Scotland and Scotsmen of the Eighteenth Century*, i (Edinburgh, 1888), 468). Some of Smith's other feats of absent-mindedness such as walking into a tan-pit while expatiating on the division of labour and, during a breakfast conversation, crumbling his bread into the tea-pot and pouring water on it, only to declare that 'it was the worst tea he had ever met with', helped to earn him a reputation for eccentricity.

[26] See n. 9.

[27] The only puzzling aspect of this influence of Desnitsky upon Catherine is that it has gone almost completely unnoticed. For some time, indeed, I was under the impression that it had quite escaped the attention of other scholars in this field, for there is no mention of Desnitsky's influence on Catherine's *Nakaz* in the writings of the principal pre-revolutionary student of Desnitsky's works, N. M. Korkunov in his *Istoriya filosofii prava*, 5-e izd. (Spb., 1908), nor of Desnitsky's *Predstavlenie* in the most scholarly edition of the *Nakaz* (*Nakaz Imperatritsy Ekateriny II*,

No fewer than twenty-six articles of the *Nakaz* (articles 575–600) bear a definite (and, in many cases, verbatim) relationship to Desnitsky's formulations. It is true that there are also some similarities between certain of Desnitsky's points and observations to be found in the *Encyclopédie*[28] and, to a lesser extent, in Bielfeld's *Institutions politiques*.[29] Though it is doubtful whether Desnitsky drew directly from either work, it is worthy of note that Catherine borrowed from Bielfeld and the *Encyclopédie* in other articles of Chapter 22 of her *Nakaz*. There is an important distinction, however, between general similarities of view and precise verbal links. The influence of Desnitsky on Chapter 22 is even clearer than that of the cameralists or encyclopaedists, as can be illustrated by a number of examples. Traces of Smith's influence on some of Desnitsky's views adopted by Catherine will also be noted.

Desnitsky observes that 'finances may justly be divided into two main parts: (1) the expenses of the state, (2) its revenues'.[30] He recognizes four main expenses which, he states, it is necessary to formulate precisely before going on to consider taxation. The first of these concerns the personal needs of the sovereign: 'The head of the society, that is the monarch, must have the resources and preserve the appearances appropriate to his illustrious office and in accordance with his supreme power. Decorum demands that affluence and magnificence should surround his throne; but it is befitting for him, as the source of prosperity of the society, to bestow awards, encouragement, and favours, from which virtue directly increases and zeal to serve the fatherland is multiplied.'[31]

The second type of expenditure required, in Desnitsky's view, is that

dannyi kommissii o sochinenii proekta novogo ulozheniya, ed. N. D. Chechulin (Spb., 1907)). Neither Uspensky nor the more recent editors of the *Predstavlenie*, I. Ya. Shchipanov (op. cit. (n. 9)) and A. A. Zhcludkov in Pokrovsky, op. cit. (n. 5) have noted the links between the *Predstavlenie* and the *Nakaz*, and there is no mention of them in Pokrovsky's book, *Politicheskie i pravovye vzglyady S. E. Desnitskogo* (n. 1) or in a more scholarly work with the same title, P. S. Gratsiansky's unpublished Moscow University candidate's thesis of 1964. The same applies to other notable Soviet works which give a prominent place to Desnitsky, including M. T. Belyavsky's *M. V. Lomonosov i osnovanie Moskovskogo universiteta* (M., 1955, 234–51) and M. M. Shtrange, *Demokraticheskaya intelligentsiya Rossii v XVIII veke* (M., 1965, especially 193–200). Only recently, however, I have discovered valuable reinforcement of my strong conviction that a comparison of the fourth appendix to Desnitsky's *Predstavlenie* with Chapter 22 of the *Nakaz* points unmistakably to the influence of the former on the latter. It is to be found in the form of a four-page article by N. D. Chechulin published in 1913 in a *mélange* in honour of D. M. Korsakov (see N. D. Chechulin, 'Predposlednee slovo ob istochnikakh "Nakaza" ' in: *Sbornik statei v chest' Dmitriya Aleksandrovicha Korsakova* (Kazan', 1913), 22–5). Chechulin points out that he had already completed work on his edition of Catherine's *Nakaz* which appeared in 1907 when Desnitsky's *Predstavlenie* was first published in 1905. Its publication threw light on one of the two substantial sections of the *Nakaz* whose sources had previously remained a mystery to him. Chechulin does not mention Adam Smith in his 1913 article, but he firmly holds that Desnitsky's work was the source for a large section of chapter 22 of the *Nakaz* and appositely suggests that Desnitsky's exposition probably reflected lectures he had heard rather than books which he had drawn upon.

[28] See *Encyclopédie*, viii (1765), 601–4, entry on 'impôt'.
[29] Baron de Bielfeld, *Institutions politiques*, i (1760), especially 128 and 230.
[30] *Predstavlenie*, 136.
[31] Ibid. 137.

needed for guarding the internal order of the state, 'consisting of supervision over the citizens and of the execution of judgement and punishment. For that purpose, it is necessary to maintain police, town governors, officials, their subordinates, and finally the courts and their buildings.'[32]

Thirdly, Desnitsky takes account of various 'undertakings conducive to the public benefit' which 'especially in a state which has not yet been put in order, are divided into innumerable objects', among which he mentions 'the building of towns and of roads, the making of canals, the cleaning of rivers, various institutions for the education and care of the people, and various establishments capable of bringing sciences and arts into a flourishing condition'.[33]

But, finally, all this 'would be without foundation', writes Desnitsky, 'if the state did not possess defence from foreign attacks. From this it follows that it ought constantly to have various forces, both land and maritime, to build and maintain fortresses, to preserve supplies of every kind of ammunition. From this results the fourth and most important kind of state expense.'[34]

It is interesting to compare these views and priorities with those of Catherine the Great, on the one hand, and of Adam Smith, on the other. Catherine, in fact, follows Desnitsky on all four points, though whereas Desnitsky is tactful enough to give first place to the expenses required to maintain the appropriate affluence of the monarch (even though he states that his fourth point, the expense of defence of the state, is actually the most important), Catherine gives first place to defence (article 576 of the *Nakaz*) and, with reciprocal tact, accords fourth place to the personal needs of the sovereign (article 579). Her second and third points concerning internal order and public welfare (articles 577–8) follow Desnitsky both in their order and in substance. Very frequently, the correspondence between the texts is a verbatim one. Thus, on the personal needs of the sovereign (article 579 of the *Nakaz*), both Desnitsky and Catherine write: 'Decorum demands that affluence and magnificence surround the throne', from which flows 'awards, encouragement, and favours'.[35] The correspondence between Catherine's and Desnitsky's third points is likewise, in places, word for word. Catherine's version of this type of public welfare expenditure which can be compared with Desnitsky's (above) reads in full: 'Undertakings conducive to the public benefit. In this category is to be found the building of towns, the making of roads, the digging of canals, the cleaning of rivers, the establishment of schools and hospitals, and other

---

[32] *Predstavlenie*, 137. [33] Ibid. [34] Ibid.
[35] Desnitsky, ibid., and *Nakaz* (Chechulin ed. (n. 27)), 153–4. In the passage within quotation marks there is, to be precise, a difference of one word. Desnitsky speaks of *ego prestol*, whereas Catherine naturally omits the word *ego*.

innumerable objects, which the brevity of this work does not permit us to describe in detail.'[36]

A comparison of these and other points from Desnitsky's financial appendix with the lectures of Adam Smith is, unfortunately, hampered by the fact that the student notes of Smith's lectures edited by Edwin Cannan (notes now thought to have been taken in the academic year 1763–4)[37] are highly abbreviated and by the further unfortunate fact that a significant part of the final economic section of the more recently discovered (and in general very much fuller) transcript of Smith's lectures on jurisprudence is missing.[38] In a lecture delivered on 30 March 1763, Smith promised to treat the study of opulence under five headings, of which the fourth was 'Taxes or public revenue'. The extant notes, however, break off with Smith still expounding the second of his five points, that devoted to money. Yet it seems quite likely that Desnitsky was in fact following Smith in his classification of the kinds of expenses which fall to the state (and that Smith touched upon the subject in his lectures), for the first chapter of Book V of *The Wealth of Nations* is divided into four parts which are (1) 'Of the Expense of Defence'; (2) 'Of the Expense of Justice'; (3) 'Of the Expense of public Works and public Institutions'; and (4) 'Of the Expense of supporting the Dignity of the Sovereign'. Even should this be so, it must quickly be added that the comparison between Desnitsky's *Predstavlenie* and Catherine's *Nakaz*, on the one hand, and Smith's chapter 1 of Book V, on the other, cannot be taken very far, for this chapter by Smith contains some of the most brilliant sociological analysis to be found in any of his works, including an exceptionally interesting sociology of religion. This analysis has no counterpart in Catherine's works, nor in the *Predstavlenie*, though Desnitsky draws upon it (in its Glasgow lectures version) in some of his other writings.

Since the number of detailed suggestions from Desnitsky which Catherine adopts is too great for them to be discussed fully here, one or two further examples must suffice. In her discussion of the preliminary questions to be asked prior to the imposition of taxes, Catherine (articles 582–6) follows Desnitsky precisely. Her formulation reads:

1. On what objects ought taxes to be imposed?
2. How to make them least burdensome for the people?

[36] *Nakaz*, 153.

[37] See R. L. Meek and A. S. Skinner, 'The Development of Adam Smith's Ideas on the Division of Labour', *The Economic Journal*, lxxxiii (1973), 1096–7.

[38] One of the editors of the forthcoming edition of the new set of Smith's lecture notes has written: 'The new notes do not extend as far as the Cannan notes—they stop short in the middle of the economics section—but most of the material up to there is found in the new notes in greatly expanded form. My provisional hypothesis is that the new notes are a student's transcription of *shorthand* notes taken down by him in class during the 1762–3 session.' (Meek, op. cit. (n. 7), 12).

3. How to diminish the expenses of collecting taxes?
4. How to prevent frauds in the revenue?
5. How is the revenue to be administered?[39]

Several of these points made by both Desnitsky and Catherine bear a marked resemblance to Adam Smith's 'maxims with regard to taxes in general',[40] but the influence of Smith on Desnitsky, and hence on Catherine, becomes more clearly evident when we examine some of Desnitsky's and Catherine's remarks under the second of these headings.

In Catherine's version (article 590) we read: 'But in order to make the imposts less sensitively felt by the subjects, it ought at the same time to be preserved as a general rule, that in all circumstances monopolies should be avoided, that is, a privilege should not be given to anyone, exclusive of all others, to trade in this or that commodity.'[41]

Desnitsky, after making a strong attack on the practice of tax-farming, sums up his discussion of this point thus: '. . . in order, as far as possible, to make the imposts made upon the subjects not sensitively felt, it is necessary to preserve as general rules: (1) in all circumstances to avoid monopolies; (2) not to impose internal duties on any kind of goods; (3) when tax-farmers are to be found, to exercise extremely rigorous supervision over them'.[42]

It is not only in Adam Smith's celebrated hostility to monopoly that Desnitsky has followed his Glasgow teacher. All three of Desnitsky's 'general rules' were ones upon which Smith laid very great stress. On the first of the three points, the published notes of Smith's lectures taken by a student contemporary of Desnitsky are sufficiently eloquent: '. . . monopolies . . . destroy public opulence. . . . When only a certain person or persons have the liberty of importing a commodity, there is less of it imported than would otherwise be; the price of it is therefore higher, and fewer people supported by it. . . . In monopolies, such as the Hudson's Bay and East India companies, the people engaged in them make the price what they please . . . exclusive privileges of corporations have the same effect. The butchers and bakers raise the price of their goods as they please, because none but their own corporation is allowed to sell in the market, and therefore their meat must be taken, whether good or not.'[43]

On the question of internal duties, Smith commented in his lectures: 'In the method of levying our customs we have an advantage over the French. Our customs are all paid at once by the merchants, and goods, after their entry in the custom house books, may be carried by a permit through any part of the country without molestation and expense,

[39] *Nakaz*, 154.
[40] *The Wealth of Nations* (n. 23), ii, 350–1.
[41] *Nakaz*, 155.
[42] *Predstavlenie*, 140.
[43] Smith, *Lectures on Justice, Police, Revenue and Arms* (n. 14), 179–80.

except some trifles upon tolls, etc. In France a duty is paid at the end of almost every town they go into, equal if not greater, to what is paid by us at first; inland industry is embarrassed by theirs, and only foreign trade by ours.'[44]

Smith follows these remarks immediately with some observations relevant to Desnitsky's suspicions of tax-farmers: 'We have another advantage in levying our taxes by commission, while theirs (France's) are levied by farm, by which means not one half of what they raise goes into the hands of the government . . . the rest goes for defraying the expense of levying it, and for the profit of the farmer.'[45] In *The Wealth of Nations*, Smith writes: 'Even a bad sovereign feels more compassion for his people than ever can be expected from the farmers of his revenue. He knows that the permanent grandeur of his family depends upon the prosperity of his people, and he will never knowingly ruin that prosperity for the sake of any momentary interest of his own. It is otherwise with the farmers of his revenue, whose grandeur may frequently be the effect of the ruin, and not of the prosperity of his people.'[46]

Catherine sometimes introduces significant variations into formulations which are basically Desnitsky's. Discussing (articles 593–4) taxes which produce little revenue, she goes on, interrogatively, to list a number of possible reasons for this state of affairs. Much of this section of chapter 22 (for instance, article 595: 'Is it because money circulates less there than in other places?')[47] is taken verbatim from Desnitsky, and only at the end of the section is there any substantive variation. Articles 598–9 ask whether the deficiencies in certain places are because 'the people there have few means of acquiring wealth; or does it proceed from laziness or from excessive oppression compared with others?'[48] Desnitsky (who makes it clearer than Catherine that when he is talking about arrears of taxation in certain places, he has in mind particular provinces of the *Russian empire*) makes no mention of laziness, but concludes by asking whether the deficiencies arise from the fact 'that the people have few means of acquiring wealth or are more oppressed than others?'[49]

Even on paper Catherine shows somewhat less concern than Desnitsky with the protection of the interests of the poorer inhabitants of the Russian empire and with ensuring that taxation is strictly proportionate to wealth. Desnitsky, in the section of his *Predstavlenie* devoted to taxes

---

[44] Ibid. 244–5.

[45] Ibid. 245. Desnitsky emerges as an equally strong opponent of tax-farming and of the privileges of the nobility in this sphere. 'The Sovereign', he writes, 'receives a known sum from the tax-farmer; but the tax-farmer for all his expenses in the course of the collection [of taxes] receives a large profit, sums which would remain with the people whenever a government gathered its revenues without a middleman. . . .' (*Predstavlenie*, 140).

[46] *The Wealth of Nations* (n. 23), ii, 435–6.

[47] *Nakaz*, 156.   [48] Ibid.   [49] *Predstavlenie*, 141.

on property, observes that such taxes can be divided into those imposed upon land and those imposed on buildings. He argues for a tax on land to be established on the basis of a reliable and precise calculation of its value, a course of action which, he suggests, would not increase the burdens upon the peasantry and upon agriculture, and he cites the example of England as sufficient demonstration of this. A tax on buildings in general would be even more useful, Desnitsky argues, in view of the fact that it is fixed 'according to the amount of wealth of the citizen and the fact that the lower sort of people are free from these taxes'.[50] In his discussion of the problem of how to make taxes least burdensome for the people, Desnitsky goes on to remark: 'It is true that every citizen receives equal protection from the government, but great inequality is to be found in their condition with respect to property. Thus, prudence and justice demand that, if possible, taxes should be established in accordance with this inequality of condition, and, if one may so put it, that they be adjusted in geometrical progression.'[51]

Catherine is less explicit than Desnitsky about the nature of property taxation and the principle of proportionality does not appear in the *Nakaz* in so precise a form as Desnitsky's '*po geometricheskoi progressii*'. The article of the *Nakaz* which is explicitly devoted to taxes on property and which may be compared with the passages from Desnitsky cited above reads: 'Taxes which are considered the least burdensome are those which are paid voluntarily and without constraint, which affect all the state inhabitants in general, and which increase in relation to the degree of luxury of each (*po mere roskoshi vsyakogo*)' (article 589).[52]

Desnitsky's advocacy of a tax upon buildings has no counterpart in the *Nakaz*, nor for that matter in the published version of Adam Smith's *Lectures*, though his remarks upon the land tax and upon egalitarian principles of taxation are fully in accord with Smith's views.[53] The specific advantages of land taxes mentioned by Smith are, firstly, that they are levied without any great expense, and, secondly, that they do not tend to raise the price of commodities, as the tax 'is not paid in proportion to the corn and cattle, but in proportion to the rent'.[54] In

---

[50] *Predstavlenie*, 138.

[51] Ibid. 140.

[52] *Nakaz*, 155. Articles 631–2 (p. 162) may also be related to the principles enunciated by Desnitsky.

[53] In *The Wealth of Nations* Smith discusses 'Taxes upon the Rent of Houses' at some length (op. cit. (n. 23), ii, 366–73) and it is entirely possible that he also paid attention to this form of revenue from taxation in his Glasgow lectures, since (as has been mentioned) neither of the surviving sets of student notes of these lectures is a complete record of what Smith said.

[54] Smith, *Lectures on Justice, Police, Revenue and Arms* (n. 14), 240–1. Smith also observes (p. 240): 'In France . . . land, stock, and money are there all taxed in the same manner. Of these three only land is taxed in England, because to tax the other two has some appearance of despotism, and would greatly enrage a free people. Excepting the land tax, our taxes are generally upon commodities, and in these there is a much greater inequality than in the taxes on land possession.'

The Wealth of Nations, if not in the published *Lectures*, Smith lays considerable stress on the principle of proportionality. He summarizes 'the
four maxims with regard to taxes in general' as (1) equality; (2) cer-
tainty; (3) convenience of payment; and (4) economy in collection.
Under the heading of equality, he argues: 'The subjects of every state
ought to contribute towards the support of the government, as nearly
as possible, in proportion to their respective abilities; that is, in proportion to the revenue which they respectively enjoy under the protection
of the state. The expense of government to the individuals of a great
nation is like the expense of management to the joint tenants of a great
estate, who are all obliged to contribute in proportion to their respective interests in the estate. In the observation or neglect of this maxim
consists what is called the equality or inequality of taxation.'[55]

Desnitsky's *Predstavlenie* is an altogether more concrete set of proposals
for reform than Catherine's *Nakaz* and this is nowhere more evident
than in a comparison of their observations on suitable objects of taxation. Though article 588 follows Desnitsky word for word on the five
objects on which taxes are normally laid ((1) persons; (2) property;
(3) domestic natural products used by the people; (4) goods exported
and imported; and (5) deeds), Catherine elaborates less fully on each
of these objects than does Desnitsky.[56] Thus, article 591, which is the
only one which Catherine devotes to the third of the above-mentioned
categories, is confined to some brief references to trifling imposts where
the duty is not worth the expense of collecting it, and there is no mention of the salt and liquor duties which were an important part of the
state revenues. (In 1767 the liquor tax produced 24·9 per cent and the
salt tax 11·9 per cent of the state revenues.)[57] Desnitsky is much more
to the point. He rules out grain as an object of taxation under his third
heading because it is a necessity of human life and should, therefore, be
free from taxation. He holds that there thus remain three kinds of
natural product liable to taxation: salt, liquor, and tobacco.[58]

He makes clear his opposition to the raising of revenue by means of
the tax on salt, arguing that salt is necessary for food and so this is
a compulsory tax, not a voluntary one (in the way in which taxes on
less essential commodities could be held to be). At the same time it is
a tax which bears especially heavily upon the poor, for salt is used in
equal measure by 'the nobility, merchants, the clergy, soldiers, petty
officials and foreigners, as by the peasants'. Liquor and tobacco, on the
other hand, are in large part luxuries and so more appropriate objects
of taxation than other things.[59]

[55] *The Wealth of Nations* (n. 23), ii, 350.   [56] Cf. *Nakaz*, 154–6 with *Predstavlenie*, 138–9.
[57] S. M. Troitsky, 'Finansovaya politika russkogo absolyutizma vo vtoroi polovine XVII
i XVIII vv.' in: N. M. Druzhinin (ed.), *Absolyutizm v Rossii* (M., 1964), 313. See also
N. D. Chechulin, *Ocherki po istorii russkikh finansov v tsarstvovanie Ekateriny II* (Spb., 1906),
especially 254–62.   [58] *Predstavlenie*, 138–9.   [59] Ibid. 139.

In this case also Desnitsky's views, while they are not identical to those of Adam Smith, are on essentials in line with Smith's arguments. Smith argues that 'taxes upon luxuries have no tendency to raise the price of any other commodities except that of the commodities taxed. Taxes upon necessaries, by raising the wages of labour, necessarily tend to raise the price of all manufactures, and consequently to diminish the extent of their sale and consumption.'[60] Elsewhere he writes: 'It must always be remembered . . . that it is the luxurious and not the necessary expense of the inferior ranks of people that ought ever to be taxed.'[61] He notes that in Great Britain the principal taxes upon 'the necessaries of life' are those upon salt, leather, soap, and candles and argues that such taxes 'must increase somewhat the expense of the sober and industrious poor, and must consequently raise more or less the wages of their labour'.[62] On the other hand, 'the different taxes which in Great Britain have in the course of the present century been imposed upon spiritous liquors, are not supposed to have had any effect upon the wages of labour'. An additional tax of three shillings upon a barrel of strong beer had 'not raised the wages of common labour in London'.[63] In putting 'spiritous liquors' in a different category from salt, Desnitsky is, however, anticipating these views of Smith's expressed in *The Wealth of Nations* and disagreeing with those which he heard Smith expound in his Glasgow lectures. In the *Lectures*, Smith argues that taxes 'upon industry, upon leather, and upon shoes, which people grudge most, upon salt, beer, or whatever is the strong drink of the country' all tend to diminish a nation's opulence. 'Man is an anxious animal,' Smith observes in this context, 'and must have his care swept off by something that can exhilarate the spirits. It is alleged that this tax upon beer is an artificial security against drunkenness, but if we attend to it, [we will find] that it by no means prevents it.'[64]

The links between Adam Smith, Desnitsky, and Catherine II have been stressed in this work in view of the fact that they have up to now remained virtually unknown. A number of contemporary Russian writers[65] have contrasted Desnitsky's *Predstavlenie* with Catherine's *Nakaz* in general terms and have rightly pointed to the much greater radicalism

---

[60] *The Wealth of Nations* (n. 23), ii, 402.

[61] Ibid. 418.   [62] Ibid. 403.   [63] Ibid. 401.

[64] *Lectures on Justice, Police, Revenue and Arms* (n. 14), 179. As if concerned to rebut his earlier view, Smith writes in *The Wealth of Nations*: 'Under necessities . . . I comprehend, not only those things which nature, but those things which the established rules of decency have rendered necessary to the lowest rank of people. All other things I call luxuries; without meaning by this appellation, to throw the smallest degree of reproach upon the temperate use of them. Beer and ale, for example, in Great Britain, and wine, even in the wine countries, I call luxuries. A man of any rank may, without any reproach, abstain totally from tasting such liquors. Nature does not render them necessary for the support of life; and custom nowhere renders it indecent to live without them.' (op. cit. (n. 23), ii, 400.)

[65] See, for example, M. T. Belyavsky, *Krest'yanskii vopros v Rossii nakanune vosstaniya E. I. Pugacheva* (M., 1965), 171–2; and P. S. Gratsiansky, op. cit. (n. 27), especially p. 133.

of the former. They appear, however, to have overlooked the influence of Desnitsky upon a specific section of the *Nakaz*. In accepting some of the proposals of a young and (at the time) unknown Russian scholar, Catherine was almost certainly unaware that she was also partly following the advice of a European theorist who was to become as renowned as any of the French encyclopaedists and more famous than any of the German cameralists to whom she had consciously turned for instruction. If, however, Adam Smith's direct and lasting influence upon the thought of Desnitsky and his indirect influence over some of the formulations in chapter 22 of Catherine's *Nakaz* may be regarded as beyond doubt, this should in no way detract from the significance of Desnitsky himself.

In his financial proposals, more than in other sections of his *Predstavlenie*, Desnitsky transmits a number of Smith's ideas. But even here, as to a greater extent elsewhere, he develops many points independently. His *Predstavlenie* as a whole is a work remarkable for its coherence, for the understanding of the weaknesses of the Russian political and social structure which it displays, and for its radical reformism, albeit a radicalism tempered by prudential considerations of a kind which could scarcely be absent from a work addressed to the Empress in the prevailing conditions of autocracy. Most of Desnitsky's proposals proved to be far ahead of their time in so far as their institutional realization was concerned. Thus, to take as an example legal reform, the independent judicial system, equality before the law, and trial by jury which Desnitsky advocated in this work of 1768 were not officially proclaimed until 1864 and even then they were only very imperfectly realized in practice. Not surprisingly, such proposals as Catherine II accepted even in principle from Desnitsky were from his maxims concerning taxation and economic administration rather than from among the numerous suggestions in the *Predstavlenie* aimed at reducing the power of the nobility and, in the longer term, of the autocrat herself.

Richard Cobden's Sojourn in Russia, 1847

By SERGIUS YAKOBSON

FOR Richard Cobden 1846 and 1847 were years of travel. Fourteen months were spent on the continent of Europe—in France, Spain, Italy, Germany, and Austria—with his wife, Kate. When she returned home in August 1847, he spent the final six weeks alone in Russia.

In letters to some of his associates, written before his departure from England, Cobden defined his journey as 'a private agitating tour', during which he hoped to act as 'the first ambassador from the People of this country to the nations of the continent'.[1] After playing his decisive role in the passage of the Corn Bill, he felt confident that he 'could succeed in making out a stronger case for the prohibitive nations of Europe, to compel them to adopt a freer system than I had here to overturn our protective policy'.[2] Cobden was encouraged to visit Russia by Sir Roderick Murchison, the co-author of a monumental work on the geology of European Russia and 'friend and confidant of the Emperor': Cobden, he was sure, 'could exercise an important influence upon the mind of Nicholas'. Russia was high on the list of countries to be visited. Indeed, so great was Cobden's anxiety to get there that Madrid, Vienna, Berlin, and Paris were thought of only as stages on his journey.

Russia's economic strength, her position in the world, and especially her future influence on developments outside her frontiers, were of great concern to Cobden as a public figure, as a member of parliament, and as author of a pamphlet entitled *Russia*. In this pamphlet, written in 1836, he had contended that it was the primitive Ottoman Empire, and not the more advanced Russian monarchy, that was inimical to British interest and Europe's welfare. His ideas evoked great interest and controversy at the time, although Cobden had somewhat vague notions about many of the developments taking place in 'the land of the

---

[1] His actual plans, however, were to be kept 'profoundly secret'. He was afraid, to quote his own words, that 'if it were known that I started with any such design of propagandism, all the protectionists and smugglers would be plotting to thwart me, or, perhaps, some of the latter might *shoot us* on our way to Madrid. We must not therefore drop a hint about it, for the *penny-a-liners* are ready to put any scrap of news about me in the newspapers. I shall tell nobody my destination beyond Paris' (S. Schwabe, comp., *Reminiscences of Richard Cobden* (1895), 2).

[2] This and the other quotations in this paragraph are from J. Morley, *The Life of Richard Cobden*, i (1896), 408–9.

Cossacks'. To view this land with his own eyes was obviously a great challenge. Possibly some part in Cobden's decision to see Russia was played by the Marquis de Custine's famous account of 1839, which he seems to have read carefully.

During his stay in Russia, from 13 August to 25 September 1847, Cobden kept a regular daily diary. This, together with a few but detailed letters to his wife, has served as the main source in preparing the present article.[3] The diary entries are, for the most part, matter-of-fact and straightforward and contain in concise form a mass of valuable data and observations. Some of Cobden's evaluations of things seen and heard reflect his own philosophy and the English point of view, and, inevitably, some of his findings are based on opinions of people he met in Russia, who might not be regarded as unimpeachable witnesses.

Cobden entered Russia assisted by a Jewish clerk of the Russian consul in Königsberg, himself a converted Jew. The young man—a sharp fellow, who spoke several languages—was a Russian subject whose low spirits and thoughtful aspect on approaching his native country puzzled Cobden. 'It is not exactly fear that I feel', the clerk explained, 'but I do find a disagreeable sensation here (striking his breast), perhaps it is something in the air which always affects me at this spot.' This introduction to Russia was hardly encouraging, and the words of his Jewish companion might have reminded Cobden of those of the German innkeeper at Lübeck who had expressed surprise that Custine should wish to go to Russia: 'When they [Russians] arrive in Europe they have a gay, easy, contented air, like horses set free, or birds let loose from their cages: men, women, the young and the old, are all as happy as schoolboys on a holiday. [But] the same persons when they return have long faces and gloomy looks; their words are few and abrupt; their countenances full of care.'[4]

Cobden's stay in Russia proved a most gratifying, informative, and comfortable experience. Throughout his diary one can hardly trace a line of complaint. However, the prevailing spirit in Russia at the time caused a note of disillusionment to appear in a letter written to his wife from St. Petersburg towards the end of his visit. 'Not that I can complain of the want of kindness of everybody here', he wrote, 'but there is something in the air or water or the moral or intellectual atmosphere of this part of the world, which had cast a sort of languor over my feelings from which I have hardly recovered' (letter of 17 September).

[3] The diary and letters are preserved in the Department of Manuscripts of the British Museum: Add. MSS. 43674 vol. xxviii D and E (Cobden's diary) and Add. MSS. 50749 (Cobden's letters to his wife). A copy of the diary may be examined also at the West Sussex Record Office in Chichester: W.S.R.O. Cobden Papers, 454–62. Only a small portion of this material has so far appeared in print, as part of Morley's biography (n. 2). I am indebted to the Trustees of the British Museum, the Governors of Dunford House, and the County Archivist of West Sussex for their generous permission to make use of the unpublished material.
[4] Marquis de Custine, *The Empire of the Czar*, i (1843), 49 f.

Cobden failed to obtain a private audience with the Emperor; the closest he came to seeing him—'the finest man in the field'—was at a parade near the capital. Almost immediately after arriving in St. Petersburg Cobden left for the fair in Nizhny Novgorod. By the time he returned to the capital 'the great man' was preparing to leave for Moscow to review the troops. Although Cobden feared that some at home would regret this omission, he felt now at the end of his European tour 'that these presentations to royalty are mere forms' (letter of 17 September). Of the Tsar's family Cobden was invited to visit Prince Peter of Oldenburg, a cousin of the Emperor. He speaks of him as a great anglophile, full of admiration for the public spirit and moral virtues of the English, and deploring in Russia the 'two greatest evils, corruption and drunkenness'.

On the part of the government it was Count Nesselrode, the Foreign Minister, who took an interest in Cobden's visit and work. They saw each other on several occasions. At first Cobden regarded Nesselrode as a Russian Metternich, 'more an adept at finesse and diplomacy than a man of genius or of powerful talent', but a later entry in his diary contained a harsher judgement: 'A mediocre man who in England would not have risen higher than to the head of a bureau.'

It was primarily Baron Alexander (Kazimirovich) Meyendorff, the well-informed head of the Moscow Board of Trade, who acted as his friendly mentor and cicerone. Cobden was introduced to him by Meyendorff's brother, Peter, who was Russian ambassador in Berlin. Throughout Cobden's diary one repeatedly finds high praise for his assistance and efforts. 'Baron Meyendorff has proved a treasure for me', he wrote to his wife on 31 August. 'He and I are like brothers in our sympathies.'

Most of the numerous people Cobden spoke to—Russians, Britons, and other foreigners living in Russia, government and court officials, diplomats, men of affairs, members of the higher and lower nobility, merchants and teachers—turned out to be hospitable, open-hearted, and co-operative, as well as knowledgeable in their respective spheres. Cobden's knowledge of French and his easy manner toward strangers facilitated communication. His interests were wide. The Moscow historian M. P. Pogodin called on Cobden at Nizhny Novgorod and impressed him as 'an able and interesting man'. He exchanged views with A. I. Chivilev, the Moscow professor of economics, who delighted Cobden by informing him that the study of free trade ideas was included in the university curriculum. In the company of Baron Meyendorff at the English Club in Moscow, Cobden met P. A. Chaadaev, one of the most interesting figures in Russian intellectual circles of the forties. Despite the official declaration of Chaadaev as a madman, Cobden describes him as 'an intelligent, educated Russ, but somewhat dreamy'.

The diary, unfortunately, does not disclose the topic of their conversation, but their meeting evidently went well, since the following day Cobden received as a gift from Chaadaev a collection of engravings of Moscow.

The average citizen was friendly and hospitable toward Cobden. He mentions a widow, the owner of a small shop in Valday where tea, honey, home-made stockings were sold. Hearing about the English traveller, she insisted on presenting him with raspberries and bread, saying, 'You are the guest of the Emperor and it is my duty to show you hospitality'. Another time, in a Moscow church Cobden gave a few silver coins to a poor, uneducated Russian woman, a pilgrim from Siberia, and was immediately included in her prayers. Her spontaneous response made Cobden pause for a second. 'Who can doubt the sincerity of such a devotee', he wrote, 'whatever may be our opinion of her intelligence?'

Cobden chose, or was advised, to divide his time in Russia between the two capitals and Nizhny Novgorod. St. Petersburg evoked mixed feelings. The view from the river Neva, with its granite embankments lined with public buildings, impressed him. 'Probably no city', he asserts in his diary, 'can boast of anything equal to it'. And to his wife he wrote, 'There is no city in Europe with so noble a stream flowing through it. Should another Liverpool one day grow up at Birkenhead, then the Mersey will alone outshine the Neva at St. Petersburg' (letter of 19 August). Strangely enough, the size of the individual squares and streets in the city disturbed him. 'The houses', he complained, 'are lost and the palaces look insignificant in such vast open spaces. Peter's Statue, on a granite rock, which would look sublime at Charing Cross or Waterloo Place, is here a diminutive looking affair. The appearance of the city altogether is that of a parvenue who has just entered fashionable life and has copied all the newest modes, but there is too much gloss and glitter generally about such imitations.'

Although personal introductions and tours of commercial and industrial sites kept Cobden busy day and night, there was time to visit the capital's famous landmarks. There was the Winter Palace, which impressed him by the 'noble proportions' of the great halls and the 'good taste' of the decorations, although he was disappointed by the dearth of rare paintings. He regretted—and this is typical of him—that the portraits were 'nearly all of soldiers'. Obviously, he had to spend some time viewing the Hermitage collections. But, despite the few Raphaels, some excellent Rembrandts and Wouwermans, he felt that on the whole they could not be compared with the collections at Dresden, Florence, or Madrid.

After a few weeks Cobden was inclined to believe that contemporary Russia was the only land still spending vast amounts of money to erect religious buildings. It was his opinion that 'Russia is in the middle age of church building, as in her civilization'. In general, he approved the style of the more recent Russian churches. He found St. Isaac's Cathedral (nearing completion after 27 years and an outlay of four million sterling) to be attractive. The Kazan' Cathedral was also 'a gorgeous church'. The practice of keeping in Russian churches keys of conquered fortresses, banners, and other war trophies, such as the baton of Marshal Davout, attracted his special attention. Among the secular buildings in St. Petersburg visited by Cobden was the Exchange, which he thought a 'noble building', but, in line with his general attitude, he voiced his regret that 'governments which erect capacious halls for the accommodation of the merchants should put every possible obstacle by their tariffs in the way of their transactions'. And the inspection of a huge, luxuriously equipped private palace of the Armenian magnate I. L. Lazarev caused him to observe sadly that 'it would be well enough to live in such a place, if we were immortal, but it is not a house to die in'.

An attaché of the British legation took Cobden to Peterhof, where he was shown the former residence of Peter the Great, his clothes, walking sticks, and some specimens of his wood handicraft. But of greater interest to him was his visit to the nearby estate of Prince Alexander Potemkin, Marshal of Nobility for St. Petersburg, which he found preserved in the style of a 'first rate English nobleman's residence'. Here, quite unexpectedly, Cobden found an intellectually refined company which, besides his host—'an amiable, quiet man'—consisted of the latter's wife 'known for her piety and good works', her sister Madame la Générale Sophie Poltoratsky, their brother Prince Andrew Golitsyn, and their cousin Countess Elizabeth Potemkin, née Trubetskoy. Members of this family proved to be as friendly as they were well-informed. Cobden was pleased to find that the three Russian ladies were 'all au courant with the proceedings of our [Anti-Corn Law] League, and had read our speeches and sympathized with our movement'. Questions of Russian politics were discussed with some frankness. During the evening Madame Poltoratsky, whose 'sophisticated Parisian conversation' had charmed Custine eight years earlier in Yaroslavl',[5] again enlivened the conversation with her spirited and bold criticism of the government, which she attacked for its extravagant expenditure on the army and the annual outlay of £60,000 to maintain the imperial stables. Inadvertently the situation of the Russian serfs became the central theme of the discussion. Prince Golitsyn drew a parallel between Russia and a strong young man suffering from la vérole, where the question was 'whether the disease can be cured or whether it would turn into a case of chronic consumption'. The lady of the house assured Cobden that the 25,000 peasants owned by her and her husband were treated with the kindness

---

[5] Custine, op. cit. (n. 4), iii. 137 ff.

of parents. He was made to visit a school which she had established for peasant children in a neighbouring village, and he was told of the resistance of their parents who suspected that the Countess had some *arrière pensée* and was secretly preparing the children for military service. Cobden's conversations left him with the impression that the *esprit de corps* of the nobles, with few exceptions, was 'raised against the Emperor who is known to be anxious to emancipate the serfs, and whose mode of procedure is regarded with disfavour by the noblesse'. Thus, no immediate change for the serfs was in sight and it seemed, for the time being at least, that it depended upon the character of the owners 'whether their dependents be utterly miserable or comparatively happy'. Cobden left this 'very pleasant family' enriched in his knowledge of the social conditions in Russia, and carrying as gifts a few religious books in French, a basket of preserves for himself, and a pair of slippers for his wife.

If the architectural splendour of St. Petersburg escaped Cobden, the peculiar style of Moscow bewildered him. 'This city', he admits, 'surprises me. I was not prepared for so interesting and unique a spectacle.' But Cobden did not avoid the common practice of drawing superficial comparisons. In Moscow, he observes, 'one might fancy himself to be in Baghdad or Granada a thousand years ago'. 'Charming', 'picturesque' are the words he uses to describe the city. For him the Kremlin is 'a picturesque cluster of palaces, churches, and monuments'. But, at the same time, he finds one of the churches there 'very grotesquely planned outside and within',[6] and the typically Russian 'cluster of cupolas of all sorts of patterns and colours' did not seem to please him. The Armoury in the Kremlin, with its collection of antiquities and curiosities, left him equally cold. These, he thought, lacked 'any intrinsic good taste or value', and their association with famous names in Russian history was 'merely of local interest up to the beginning of the last century'.

As for the social life of the city, Cobden understood that Moscow was not 'in great favour with the Emperor', since it served as a winter resort for the poorer nobility and a retreat for those dissatisfied with affairs in St. Petersburg. The men in the street struck him as 'more Asiatic in their appearance and dress than at St. Petersburg, and also more superstitious'. On the other hand, Cobden sensed the presence in Moscow society of 'an independent public spirit'. The people here, he found, were 'talking more freely than at St. Petersburg, and criticizing the government without hesitation'. In fact, he was able to trace in Moscow a party of 'Young Russians' to whom he gives special attention in his diary. 'They are called the "Slave Party", their object being to isolate the Slavonic race and allow it gradually to develop its own civilization.' These Slavophiles, he records, 'say that their rulers, from Peter the

---

[6] Cobden does not name this church, but the description suggests he may have had in mind the Cathedral of Vasily Blazhennyi, which stands near the Kremlin.

First down to the present reign, have aped European models, and neglected or perverted the original characteristics of the Russian people; they find fault with the mania for foreign politics which their sovereigns have generally displayed, and the great expense which this costs the people in large standing armaments; they complain of the neglect of internal amelioration, of the extravagance and corruption of the nobility, and the consequent oppression and impoverishment of their serfs; they regard St. Petersburg with especial disfavour as the centre of court splendour which shines with the reflected light of Paris and London. They regard Russia as all-sufficient for Russians, and entertain no aggressive or conquering propensities.' Cobden gives his own appraisal of this romantic, isolationist, pacifist and populist movement in his diary, where he writes: 'This party resembles in some respects our "Young Englanders"; both write poetry in praise of the past, both censure the present, and both would arrest the progress of the future. They are equally amiable and dreamy and insignificant.'

Nizhny Novgorod was a different proposition. Here it was the fair rather than the city itself which attracted Cobden's attention. Miles of wooden booths, constructed by the government for the use of merchants at a cost of hundreds of thousands of pounds, greeted him. These housed a great variety of merchandise, brought long distances on barges, boats, horses, and even, as far as Orenburg, on camels. At one time there were forty to fifty thousand horses waiting to transport goods changing hands in the city. The quality of the wares varied widely. While most of the printed calicos of many patterns and colours—priced as high as in England—impressed Cobden as inferior, he found the rich silks and gold cloth used by priests in church and by ladies in harems of the Orient to be of 'splendid and costly workmanship'. The iron wares offered at the fair were limited and disappointing. In spite of the high quality of Russian raw iron, the iron works—almost wholly in the hands of the crown and the nobility—did not keep pace with other industries, and the prohibition of the import of iron products made the Russian producer careless of the needs of the native consumer. Traders at the fair sought the blessing of the church for their transactions, and in the church Cobden visited he noticed that 'the ceremonies were observed with more devotion than even in the Catholic churches in Rome'. Asia played a significant role in the trade done at Nizhny Novgorod. Cobden was told that the Chinese had never attended the fair, but a 'spacious and handsome range of warehouses has been erected for the products of China, with pagoda towers and Chinese ornaments', and it was estimated that the value of the tea alone brought from China to the city exceeded a million sterling. Worshippers in the city mosque belonged to 'a great variety of physiognomy': Tatars, Persians, and men from Bokhara and Khiva.

Travel by stage coach and similar transportation (the railway between St. Petersburg and Moscow was not opened until 1851) was a rewarding experience. It permitted Cobden to observe closely the lives of ordinary Russians outside the main cities, to see them at work and play, and to talk to them if only through an interpreter. The urgent need for such personal contacts is well demonstrated by the revelation in his diary in the fifth week of his stay in Russia that 'it is curious to find in Russia a civilized taste for dancing, music, flowers and tea'.

The flat countryside of western and central Russia—with only a few slight elevations and a view mostly constricted by the straight lines of fir forests—did not appeal to him. He found the landscape monotonous, dull, and even oppressive. He had travelled from Tilsit to Nizhny Novgorod, he complained, without discovering a mile 'which required a drag chain to the wheel or where the horses could not trot' (letter to his wife, 17 September). The Russian people intrigued and puzzled him. Obviously, he felt it was a strange and often bizarre world to which he was suddenly exposed. At the English Club in Moscow, although the majority of members were of Russian stock, Cobden felt practically at home: 'A very fine establishment,' he commented, 'fit to be compared with anything in London.' A large Moscow tea-drinking establishment with all the waiters dressed in white linen smocks and trousers was a less familiar sight. But his experience at the public gardens in provincial Torzhok where people came to hear music and promenade was quite unrealistic. Indeed, he devoted a whole page of his diary to a description of the rich and unusual costumes worn by the ladies there, which he priced as high as £80. Was it a *bal masqué* or an opera, he asked. The effect of these attires, he observed to his wife (letter of 17 September), 'was so oriental and glowing that had the fair ones been a little prettier I should have almost fancied myself in the gardens of the Grand Sultan whilst the inmates of the harem were taking their exercise'.

The peasants on the road from St. Petersburg to Moscow struck him as 'physically a very fine race'. The men's attire seemed to give them 'quite an oriental look', although the high-brimmed low hat appeared to him to be imported from Andalusia. Later, the peasants he saw between Moscow and Nizhny Novgorod had a 'more degraded aspect', and this time their high-crowned hats, brown and misshapen, possessed an 'Irish aspect'. Cobden preferred the look of the Russian men to the women. The full flowing garments and long beards of the male peasants, he thought, gave them a noble expression. He was inclined to agree with previous travellers that Russian 'women have a very inferior appearance to the men'. 'As a rule,' he reported to his wife (letter of 17 September), 'they are downright ugly. I have seen few good-looking women of any rank in Russia. The peasant women have a fashion of tying the waist strings of their dresses *above* their bosoms which hang down, where English women like to have a small waist. It is impossible to conceive anything so ugly.' One humorous interpretation of this unbecoming fashion, which Cobden elicited, was that the priests had prescribed it to prevent men from falling into temptation.

Cobden was impressed by the display of benevolence on the part of the villagers, who greeted criminals who passed their dwellings under escort with bread, provisions, and even money. He accepted the explanation that this was common practice and that 'on their arrival in Siberia the criminals have always a little stock of money in hand, and . . . everything given is put in the hands of one of the prisoners who is a banker for all'. On the other hand, Cobden's sense of justice and decency was momentarily hurt when he saw male and female serfs being transported to Siberia ostensibly for the crime of 'ill-temper'—i.e. having failed to please their masters. But two weeks later, when writing to his wife about the episode (letter of 17 September), his feelings had already been 'much mitigated', and this for two reasons. Firstly, because he had learned that 'it is a common thing to plead guilty to insubordination when there are worse charges laid against them'. And secondly, because his vision of Siberia had by now undergone a remarkable change. 'It seems from all accounts to be that part of Russian empire,' he writes, 'where the population is the most independent. There are no serfs in Siberia; the people are all proprietors. They consider themselves superior to the Russians, and as there is plenty of good land unoccupied, every fresh emigrant is valued as an acquisition. It is only the murderers or other great criminals who are treated with severity when they arrive there.'

The standards of agriculture practised in nineteenth-century Russia took Cobden back into history, and he sharply censured them as unworthy of modern times. 'The ploughs', he observed, 'were constructed upon the model of those in use a thousand years ago. The scythes and reaping hooks might have been the implements of the ancient Scythians. The spades in the hands of the peasants were either entirely of wood or merely tipped with iron. The fields were yielding scarcely a third of the crop of grain which an English farmer would derive from similar land. There was no science traceable in the manuring or cropping of the land, no intelligence in the improving of the breed of the cattle, and I could not help asking myself by what perversity of judgement an agricultural people could be led to borrow from England its newest discoveries in machinery for spinning cotton, and to reject the lessons which it offered for the improvement of that industry upon which the wealth and strength of the Russian empire so preeminently depend.'

Cobden's direct contact with the Russian people was fairly short, but it was sufficient for him to reach a basic and important conclusion.

'We are quite under a delusion', he wrote from St. Petersburg at the end of his visit, 'as to the character of the Russian peasantry. We think them a savage, warlike, conquering race, anxious only to escape from the northern regions and to pour like the Goths upon the other countries of Europe. Nothing can be more absurd. They are a mild, tractable, quiet people, attached to their country and their villages, proud of Russia and loving its climate; the winter, with its dry frosts and its sledges, being to them far preferable to the wet and dirty weather of southern regions. They are not warlike and quarrelsome. On the contrary, the army is most unpopular with the peasantry who, when they leave their villages to become soldiers, are followed with the tears and lamentations of their neighbours. They have tastes which bespeak their amiable social tendencies. . . . I can hardly help being in love with people who are addicted to tea drinking two or three times a day' (letter of 17 September).

Cobden came to Russia primarily as a free trade advocate, and he missed no opportunity to debate and advance his ideas, which he believed had universal validity.

Upon his arrival at the Russian frontier at Tauroggen he raised the question of the merits of the high protective system in Russia with the head of the customs house, his assistants, and an army colonel; all were against it, since in their opinion high protective duties were only intended to favour a few manufacturers, many of whom were foreigners and, after all, not prosperous. Adherents of Cobden's ideas—the civil governor of Moscow 'de Kapnist', the Councillor of State Fomin, and Alexander Butovsky, author of a three-volume work on the people's economy—succeeded in gaining introductions to the famous man. In a letter preserved at Chichester,[7] Butovsky thanks the master for the great moral support given him during their conversation. But Cobden sought to reach others—his opponents, the doubters, the men in power, to present and clarify his ideas, to promote discussion and thus influence future developments. People to whom he spoke reacted differently. Some advanced serfdom, the 'rude and barbarous state of the country', and the shortage of roads as reasons against the acceptance of the system he favoured. The Minister of Finance, F. P. Vronchenko, to whom he delivered a half hour's speech on free trade without interruption, 'was willing to learn. He listened like a man of good common sense, and his observations were very much to the point.' Cobden's new friend, Baron Meyendorff, seemed to be favourably disposed to a 'gradual relaxation of the [protective] system'. A general, 'an honest man and a protectionist', favoured the protection of native industry in its initial stages. The English manager of a large spinning mill, owned

7 W.S.R.O. Cobden Papers, 2.

by a joint stock company in St. Petersburg, firmly declared that 'without the protecting duty against English yarn he could not carry on the mill even if he paid no wages'.

Cobden addressed larger groups and gatherings. Thus, Count P. D. Kiselev, 'one of the ablest of the ministers, having the direction of the public domains', and 'other persons of rank' had a lively after-dinner discussion with him on the subject of free trade in the foreign minister's drawing room, with Count Nesselrode quietly listening to the controversy. 'My opponents', Cobden thought, 'were moderate in their pretensions, and made a stand only for the protection of industries in their *infancy*. All parties threw overboard cotton spinning as an exotic which ought not to be encouraged in Russia.' A banquet was given in Cobden's honour on one of the islands in St. Petersburg almost on the eve of his departure, attended by some 200 persons, including leading government officials, foreign merchants, and a sprinkling of diplomats. It was a pleasant occasion and a debate developed between him and one of his 'old Chartist persecutors'. 'Nothing of the sort was ever seen before', he wrote to his wife (letter from Travemünde, 29 September), and in his diary he recorded that 'an Englishman named Hodgson, manager of Loader's spinning mill, who was formerly a Radical orator in England, addressed the meeting pretty much in the style of some of my old Chartist opponents in England, which afforded me an opportunity of replying to him greatly to the satisfaction of the meeting'. But most pleasing to Cobden was the 'freedom of speech and absence of restraint which pervaded the meeting, and which contrasted with the timidity I have sometimes seen in Italy and Austria'.

Cobden could well be pleased with his efforts. 'A free trade debate in Nesselrode's drawing room', he remarked, with irony and self-satisfaction, 'must at least have been a novelty.' The future, as well, looked promising. 'The tide of opinion has turned here,' he told his wife, 'and we shall see the government gradually proceed in the direction of commercial freedom. I have far more hopes of speedy changes in Russia than in France or Spain. This is a country with which England may have an increasing trade. There is a vast field of production. The whole country is a plain surface, capable of cultivation, with some of the finest rivers in the world to aid the internal commerce.' Cobden's faith was further strengthened by news of a revelation made by the late Minister of Finance, Count E. F. Kankrin, an active champion of the high protective system in Russia. In private conversation with a junior Russian official Kankrin said that 'he had laid on high duties upon foreign products against his better judgement, at the instance of powerful and interested parties, and that he hoped to live long enough to change the system' (letter of 17 September).

During his sojourn in Russia Cobden, himself a calico printer, devoted considerable time to gathering information on the state of Russia's textile industry. He visited several mills and endeavoured to elicit pertinent facts from owners, managers, and financiers. His diary does not summarize his findings, and this could hardly have been expected. But many entries in which he gives his professional appraisal of some of the developments and discusses the problems of the people involved are still of considerable interest to a student of the Russian economy. Only a few can be mentioned here.

At the time the Russian textile industry was experiencing growing pains typical of early development. Primitive weaving on hand looms was still practised in the villages. The peasants, free from tilling the land during the long winter months, devoted much of their time to such pursuits in search of additional income. This was a purely Russian affair. Many of the technologically advanced mills located in and around Moscow were owned by foreigners. Owners from the ranks of the Russian nobility were basically uninterested and ill-prepared for managing their factories. Floating capital was in short supply and, in many instances, they were heavily indebted to the bankers. Furthermore, they were inclined to live in grandiose style beyond their means, and preferred residing in St. Petersburg or abroad. Unable to cope with the business themselves, they sought help from foreigners, often Englishmen, whom they employed as mill managers and who were paid salaries as high as £1,000 a year. The untrained labour force, it was said, required twice as much time to do the same job as operatives in England. Such low performance, however, was not necessarily typical of Russian workmen. For instance, an English manager of a railway shop, administered at the time by three Americans in St. Petersburg, told Cobden that the Russian artisan was 'very quick in learning his business and easily managed. When he entered upon the undertaking he was told the Russians could be controlled only by blows, but finds that a system of rewards answers better than punishments. He speaks of them as amiable and mild in their character, and disturbances and quarrels are unknown amongst them, but they are addicted to petty pilfering.'

Of the more successful establishments Cobden saw the following (some of which were still in operation in 1917) deserve attention:

A large spinning mill in St. Petersburg, owned by a joint stock company, and containing 65,000 spindles. The steam engine operated for 75 hours a week (13 hours a day for five days, and 10 hours on Saturday). In addition to Sundays, there were 18 further days observed as holidays each year.

A large cotton-print works in Moscow belonging to the Prokhorov family. Cobden observed that the prices for the prints were 50 per cent higher than in England. The steam boilers were heated with wood and turf. The labour force consisted of 600 crown serfs, 300 seignorial serfs, and 200 'free burgesses' (evidently *meshchane*) of Moscow. Cobden was told that these 'different classes work together without any feelings of caste'. He was pleased to notice that the proprietors of this establishment took 'some pains with the education of the young people', and when he saw the workers engaged in praying and singing before dinner, he found it 'very sweet and touching'.

The Moscow factory of the Guchkovs, who were Old Believers and 'energetic men' and the second largest employers of labour in Russia. They were primarily engaged in the production of silk, worsted, and other materials. The mill in Moscow had 3,000 hands; in addition to the adults (all serfs) some boys worked there who had been taken on from the foundling hospital. The Guchkovs lived in 'greater style than a similar class in England'. For instance, in their hot house which was a quarter of a mile long they cultivated a large variety of tropical plants at great expense.

Finally, in Cobden's eyes the best managed cotton mill in the country, which had 13,500 spindles and two steam engines totalling 80 horsepower. This busy mill was located on a beautiful site ten miles from the city and belonged to a Moscow nobleman, Colonel Volkov. It was run by an Englishman and employed 1500 people who worked in shifts day and night. The steam engines were halted for only 24 hours each week, from 5.0 a.m. on Sunday until the same time the following day. Here too, the entire labour force, including the 'several well dressed respectable looking men at the desk' in the counting house, were serfs belonging to the mill. The manner in which the younger Volkov, who conducted Cobden around the premises, used the words, 'Oui, ils sont tous à nous', deeply offended Cobden. He included the following— unusual for him—bitter tirade in his diary: 'There was something coarse and repugnant in the manner in which the young man spoke of his human chattels. Serfdom appears doubly unnatural when associated with the processes of mechanical skill, so peculiarly the product of the present age. It seems like the forced union of the barbarism of the thirteenth century with the civilization of our day. When serfs are employed upon the land they have their rights to the share of its products, and they are born with a title to a subsistence upon the soil which they cultivate, partly for their own and partly for the proprietor's benefit. But here there is no such reciprocity of rights. Nor do I think that the system can be permanently maintained under such circumstances.'

Serfdom obviously greatly impeded the political and social development of Russia, which genuinely interested Cobden. But the whole state apparatus impressed him as imperfect. True, the size of the realm was a great handicap for efficient administration. Cobden relates the incident of an American fur-trader who intruded into Russian territory in North America with 80 to 100 men and three pieces of artillery. The news caused consternation, first in Irkutsk and then in the capital. No action was taken, however, since the dispatch of troops there—one year's journey from St. Petersburg—was beyond the means of the government. Other signs of maladministration came to Cobden's attention. 'In no other country in Europe', he asserts, 'except Turkey are the laws so imperfectly executed.' Indeed, he says, 'ukases are often little more than waste paper'. Although he had a poor opinion of Count Nesselrode, he reported that the heads of departments were 'all enlightened and able men'. But corruption among civil servants was rampant, and second-rate people filled the ranks of the bureaucracy. As for the Emperor, Cobden understood that he was anxious to rule the country well, but his great shortcoming was his disposition 'to regulate everything in his empire, great and small. If a bridge is to be built at St. Petersburg or Kiev, he decides on the plan. If a railroad be ordered from the capital to Moscow, he draws a straight line on the map regardless of the wants of intermediate towns, or the obstacles of the country through which it is to pass. Not a church can be erected but he must decide the form of the cupola. He regulates the shape of a soldier's cap, and marshals the nurses at a christening of one of his children. He is at once the head of the church, commander-in-chief, finance minister, president of the board of trade, secretary of state for foreign affairs and for the interior. . . . As he undertakes to direct and control every detail of the administration there is no one responsible for any department as in constitutional states.'

Apathy permeated all strata of the population. Russian members of the English Club in Moscow, having dined, proceeded straight away to the card tables, billiard rooms, or skittles. 'There is no intellectual society,' Cobden lamented, 'no topic of general interest is discussed—an un-idea'd party.' Even the horse races at Tsarskoe Selo lacked 'life and animation'.

With regard to one particular sphere of government policy, Cobden's notes are somewhat contradictory. That a Protestant was permitted to be Russian foreign minister he regarded as proof of 'the tolerance of the government in religious matters . . . worthy of imitation'. Other pages of the diary provide contrary evidence, however, in references to the persecution of sectarians, the prohibition of foreign editions of the scriptures by the state, and instances of anti-Jewish administrative practice.

For the future, Cobden recorded the possibility of three 'grave difficulties' facing Russia. The emancipation of the serfs, naturally, was one. Second—and this for him was a rather unfamiliar line of speculation—the 'religious tone', at present 'one of mere unmeaning formalities' in Russia, unless aligned with the progress of ideas, threatened to become 'a cause of infidelity on the one hand, and blind bigotry on the other'. Third, the government had to guard against possible 'dangerous collisions of opinion' between the three heterogeneous elements belonging to the Russian *tiers état*—the freed serfs, the manufacturers and the bureaucracy.

Apart from these speculations, the Cobden diary contains little in the way of prediction or even generalization. This is not surprising. The primary purpose of the diary was to provide a more or less detailed record for future private use. It was to capture places he visited, conversations he had, impressions he gained as the days passed by, and his immediate response to many kinds of people and continually changing situations. And how hazardous it was even for a Russian subject to attempt to pierce the future can be seen from a forecast of Baron Alexander Meyendorff, a man Cobden respected as 'an active minded and intelligent German, possessing much statistical knowledge about Russian trade and manufactures'. It was Meyendorff's view, Cobden reported, that 'the geographical and climatical features of Russia will always prevent its being anything but a great village'.

The British Press and the Russian Revolution of 1905–1907

By W. HARRISON

THE years of the Russian revolution of 1905–7, following as they did so hard on Russia's defeats in the Russo-Japanese War, saw a shift in the international balance of power, with the growth of German might and the enfeeblement of Russia. These developments were a cause of serious concern not only to Russia's ally, France, but also to Great Britain, and it is against this background that the intense British interest in the Russian internal crisis must be considered. Some aspects of British opinion concerning the Revolution of 1905–7 have been dealt with by historians,[1] but the present study attempts a wider examination than has so far been made of British press reactions in the period between the end of the Russo-Japanese War and the signing of the Anglo-Russian Convention on 31 August 1907.

In the early months of 1905 Russia had few friends in Britain. Public opinion had been incensed by the Dogger Bank incident, when Admiral Rozhdestvensky's Baltic Squadron had attacked the Hull fishing fleet in October 1904, and all sections of British society reacted with anger and disgust to the news of Bloody Sunday, 9/22 January 1905, when troops fired on Gapon's workers' demonstration in St. Petersburg. The British press, from *Justice*, organ of the Social Democratic Federation (S.D.F.), to *The Times*, maintained a barrage of hostile criticism of the tsarist regime which caused *Novoe vremya* to protest against this 'dishonorable propaganda' (*beschestnaya agitatsiya*);[2] at the same time periodicals contributed innumerable articles which created a picture of Russia sinking in chaos, oppression, bankruptcy, and corruption.[3] Yet for all that, Russia was still viewed as a dangerous imperialist

[1] W. S. Adams, 'British Reactions to the 1905 Revolution', *Marxist Quarterly*, ii (1955), 173–86; J. O. Baylen, 'W. T. Stead and the Russian Revolution of 1905', *Canadian Journal of History*, ii (1966), 45–66; M. Beloff, 'Lucien Wolf and the Anglo-Russian entente, 1907–1914' (Jewish Historical Society of England. Lucien Wolf Memorial Lecture, 7 March 1951); E. B. Chernyak, 'Pervaya russkaya revolyutsiya i rabochee dvizhenie v Anglii i Irlandii' in: *Pervaya russkaya revolyutsiya i mezhdunarodnoe revolyutsionnoe dvizhenie* (M., 1956), 131–80.

[2] *Novoe vremya*, 16/29 Jan. 1905.

[3] e.g. E. J. Dillon's regular contributions to *The Contemporary Review*, also A. Ular, 'The Prospects of Russian Revolution' in the same journal, Feb. 1905, pp. 153–73; P. Kropotkin, 'The Constitutional Agitation in Russia' in *The Nineteenth Century and After*, Jan. 1905, pp. 27–45, and E. J. Dillon's 'The Breakdown of Russian Finances', ibid., March 1905, pp. 373–89. An anonymous article in *The National Review* entitled 'The End of Autocracy' (issue for May, pp. 416–46) depicted the Tsar as mentally sick.

enemy, a threat to India and Scandinavia.[4] Only the downfall of the tsarist system and the creation of a constitutional regime would render Russia acceptable as a civilized power. This was the general state of British opinion up to the beginning of the peace talks at Portsmouth in August 1905, but already there had been straws in the wind, which betokened a possible change in British attitudes. Japanese victories, it was realised, were not an unmixed blessing: the victory of a yellow race over a European might have serious repercussions for other imperial powers; and it served to weaken Russia as a counterweight to Germany. Britain and France needed Russia in Europe, and, as the *Westminster Gazette* declared on 6 June, 'The politics of Europe are such that we cannot be both anti-Russian and anti-German at the same time.'

Thus, by the end of the Russo-Japanese War many minds in Britain were turning towards the prospect of better relations with Russia. It was known that official circles in Britain were anxious for an accommodation, and King Edward had sent a draft of terms for a possible agreement to Witte on the latter's return from Portsmouth.[5] Speculation on the subject was growing in the press, and it was felt that a great opportunity was at hand. On 1 October, for example, the *Observer* wrote, 'If at the end of the next ten years an entente with Russia has not been arrived at then diplomacy will have failed.' But if sections of British public opinion were moving towards thoughts of an entente, for most people in Britain any real improvement in relations must wait on reform in Russia.

British interest in Russia's internal affairs was therefore acute, and for a brief period following the Tsar's manifesto, and *ukaz* of 6/19 August, which announced arrangements for the consultative 'Bulygin' Duma, there were hopes in Britain that Russia was indeed embarking on the path of reform. *The Times* examined the proposed constitution in leading articles and pronounced that despite its shortcomings it could begin the necessary process of political education in Russia.[6] The general view of the Bulygin Duma was, in the words of the *Westminster Gazette*, that it was 'a beginning and an opportunity'.[7] But these hopeful prospects were soon obscured by the spreading disorders and strikes in October, particularly by the Armenian–Tatar massacres in the Caucasus. A *Times* leader of 26 October, entitled 'The Russian Crisis', compared the Russian situation with the preliminaries of the French Revolution, and the *Observer*, which on 22 October had seen hopeful signs of improvement in Russia, declared a week later, 'There can be no treating with

4 *Manchester Guardian*, 30 Jan. 1905; Sir Cecil Spring-Rice, *The Letters and Friendships of Sir Cecil Spring-Rice: a Record*, ed. S. Gwynne (1929), i, 460; *Observer*, 12 March 1905, p. 4; *Blackwood's Edinburgh Magazine*, April 1905, p. 560.

5 S. B. Fay, *The Origins of the World War* (New York, 1947), 214.

6 *The Times*, 19, 21 Aug. 1905.

7 *Westminster Gazette*, 19 Aug. 1905.

a people in the throes of revolution, or with a Governmental regime which is about to be swept away.'[8]

In truth, there was a widespread conviction in Britain that the tsarist regime was too inefficient and corrupt to survive and from the present struggle the liberals of the Liberation movement and the *zemstva* would emerge victorious, a conviction strengthened by the vast number of articles and books on Russia published in recent months.[9] The prospect of witnessing elemental upheavals was attracting an increasing number of commentators from Britain to the Tsar's domains and there can be no doubt that the majority of British correspondents were firmly on the side of the Liberation movement. This was certainly true of the interim representative of *The Times*, Robert Wilton, who was on close terms with I. V. Gessen, soon to become a member of the central committee of the Constitutional Democratic (Kadet) Party. Indeed, Wilton was known to leave his correspondence in Gessen's charge.[10] The *Manchester Guardian's* correspondent, Harold Williams, was a friend of P. B. Struve, at whose home in Stuttgart in 1904 he had met his future wife, Ariadne Tyrkova, later also a member of the Kadet central committee.[11] And it was at a meeting arranged by Madame Petrunkevich that Bernard Pares first met Williams, the Petrunkeviches also being prominent in the liberal movement.[12] It was mostly in these radical liberal circles that British commentators in Russia found inspiration and gained much of their information, though some, like H. W. Nevinson, who arrived in Russia in November 1905 as correspondent of the *Daily Chronicle*, found most of their friends amongst the adherents of the Left, in his case, the Social Democrats.[13] On the other side were the *Daily Telegraph's* E. J. Dillon, friend of Witte, and Maurice Baring, who had arrived from Manchuria where he represented the *Morning Post*. But, although Baring was a friend of the Benckendorfs, one of whom was Russian ambassador in London, his correspondence was not sympathetic to the Russian authorities and was often strongly pro-Kadet.

Of all prominent British journalists the most favourably disposed towards Nicholas II and his regime was W. T. Stead, Radical though he was. He too had arrived at the end of August, intent on trying to bring about a reconciliation between the Russian authorities and the

[8] *Observer*, 29 Oct. 1905, p. 4.

[9] These included: Leo Deutsch, *Sixteen Years in Siberia* (1905); Hugo Ganz, *The Downfall of Russia* (1904); Father G. Gapon, *The Story of my Life* (1905); Carl Joubert, *Russia as it really is* (1904), *The Truth about the Tsar and the Present State of Russia* (1905), and *The Fall of Tsardom* (1905); P. N. Milyukov, *Russia and her Crisis* (1905); Alexander Ular, *Russia from Within* (1905). All of these books and many others were reviewed and discussed in the British press during 1905.   [10] *History of The Times*, iii, 485.

[11] A. Tyrkova-Williams, *Cheerful Giver: the Life of Harold Williams* (1935), 21–4; also her *Na putyakh k svobode* (New York, 1952), 184–6.

[12] Tyrkova-Williams, *Cheerful Giver* (n. 11), 72.

[13] H. W. Nevinson, *Fire of Life* (1935), 185.

Russian public. Although his efforts were obviously well-intentioned and attracted much attention in the Russian and British press, the general view of his mission in both countries was that it was hopelessly naïve.[14] *The Times* published his impressions under the title 'Russia's great new hope', but a leading article on 26 September made sarcastic references to his enthusiasm for the Duma's prospects. Bernard Pares seems to have summed up the attitude of British journalists in Russia when, in a lecture at Altrincham, he opined that once autocracy was beaten, misunderstandings between Britain and Russia would disappear.[15]

On 17/30 October, the Tsar issued his Manifesto enlarging the Duma's powers and promising revision of the electoral law and a guarantee of civil liberties. Initially the Manifesto was greeted with almost universal satisfaction in Britain. 'Of the travail of this week a new Russia has been born', wrote *The Times* on 31 October. The *Daily Telegraph* believed that 'Russia stands now at the golden moment of constructive compromise'.[16] The *Manchester Guardian* held that Russia now had a real constitution, as did even *Justice*,[17] and Jaakoff Prelooker's *Anglo-Russian*[18] said it was time to forgive and forget. The *Daily News*, most widely read of Liberal papers and usually consistent in its critical attitude to the tsarist regime, called 17/30 October a great day in the history of mankind.[19] The *Westminster Gazette*, the *Daily Express*, and the *Daily Mail* urged moderation and statesmanship on both sides, but the *Mail* did discern disquieting signs in the extreme demands of the Russian Liberals.[20] In one of the more thoughtful appraisals of the situation the *Standard* argued that the rejoicings in St. Petersburg indicated a great respect for the monarchy and that 'to exalt the advantage won was the surest way of making it enduring and fruitful'.[21] In other words, the surest way forward was to rally Russian public opinion to welcome and support the Manifesto. This view was in fact close to that of the moderate wing of the Russian liberal movement led by Dmitry Shipov, Count Heyden, A. I. Guchkov, and others who were soon to form the Union of 17 October for the very purpose of seeking a compromise with the authorities on the basis of the Manifesto. The more influential radical liberals, however, who were busy forming the Kadet party at a constituent congress when the Manifesto appeared, immediately denounced it and declared that they would continue their alliance with the revolutionary socialists.

[14] F. Whyte, *The Life of W. T. Stead* (1925), ii, 274 ff.; Baylen, op. cit. (n. 1); *Manchester Guardian*, 12 Oct. 1905.   [15] *Manchester Guardian*, 10 Oct. 1905.
[16] *Daily Telegraph*, 1 Nov. 1905.
[17] *Manchester Guardian*, 1 Nov. 1905; *Justice*, 4 Nov. 1905, p. 4.
[18] *The Anglo-Russian*, Nov. 1905, p. 959.
[19] *Daily News*, 1 Nov. 1905.
[20] *Daily Mail*, 1 Nov. 1905.   [21] *Standard*, 1 Nov. 1905.

This fact might have been pondered more seriously in Britain if attention had not been immediately distracted by news of riots and pogroms. *The Times* in the course of the next week carried reports of pogroms of Jews and students at Odessa, of massacres at Kishinev, of butchery at Minsk, Kazan', and Tiflis, of anarchy in Kiev. In a *Times* leader of 8 November the Russian authorities were accused of 'the cold-blooded hounding of the mob upon innocent people' and the *Daily Graphic* on the same day urged Europe to declare that 'it cannot treat as a civilized Government a body of men who appear to be lost to all sense of humanity and all sense of shame'. In general, the British press accepted that the Russian authorities were responsible for the pogroms, that this was proof of the Tsar's insincerity, and so the first bright hopes of the Manifesto had been false. An exception was the *Westminster Gazette*, which continued to urge conciliation. On 11 November it called on the reformers and revolutionary leaders: 'You have helped to make this movement and you must help to control it. . . . It was a surprise and disappointment to us that the Liberals should have refused to join Count Witte.'

The prospect of popular revolution in Russia was contemplated with satisfaction by many people in Britain, but for others it raised fears that the dissolution of the Russian empire might bring unforeseeable consequences for Europe. The *Standard,* for example, feared the spread of 'the contagion' beyond Russia's frontiers,[22] and there were rumours of possible German intervention in Poland,[23] a contingency thought to have been discussed by the Tsar and the Kaiser at Björkö in July. An article in the *Fortnightly Review*, 'Europe and the Russian Revolution' by 'Perseus', observed that the principles enunciated by the Russian liberal paper *Rus'* would make constitutional government impossible in that they denied political compromise, and it too referred to the dangers of German intervention: 'The real alternatives to Count Witte's policy of constitutional compromise and gradual reform are anarchy or the German Emperor—the dismemberment of the Russian Empire and the European Armageddon.' The same article pointed to another feature of the Russian revolution which was exercising British minds: the success of the general strike in October prompted the author to describe it as 'the most portentous and terrible instrument ever employed by political agitation'.[24]

In this atmosphere *The Times* welcomed the exercise of power by the government in arresting the St. Petersburg Soviet and in crushing the armed uprising in Moscow in December, which was described as madness and attributed to 'the Oriental part' of the Russian character.[25]

---

[22] *Standard*, 8 Nov. 1905; also *The Outlook*, 11 Nov. 1905, pp. 654–5.
[23] *Morning Post*, 15 Nov. 1905.
[24] *Fortnightly Review*, Dec. 1905, pp. 959–75.   [25] *The Times*, 20, 28 Dec. 1905.

But it would be incorrect to depict the bourgeois British press as panic-stricken at the prospect of revolution in Russia and rushing to support autocracy.[26] To British people, confident that their own Mother of Parliaments was a model suitable for all nations, the solution of the Russian crisis should be the formation of a constitutional monarchy dominated by liberals and moderates, and a Kadet victory was hoped for and expected. The Moscow rising, of which even British socialists could make little sense, seemed unlikely to lead in the direction desired by British opinion.

British public support for the actual revolution in Russia does not seem to have been strong in the second half of 1905. Early in the year an appeal by the Labour Representation Committee on behalf of Russian strikers raised almost £1,000, but an appeal for funds in aid of the revolution from the Social Democratic Federation in July limped to an embarrassing £58. 7s. 10½d. by December, a figure which *Justice* itself contrasted with £8,000 raised by the German Social Democrats.[27] On the other hand, an appeal sponsored by the Rothschilds for the victims of the pogroms reached a total of nearly £500,000,[28] and whilst it would be unrealistic to expect readers of *Justice* to compete with the Rothschilds, or even with the German Social Democratic Party, the fact remains that other appeals in *Justice* could raise £50 in a single week.[29]

Nevertheless, for the reform movement in Russia there was still very great public sympathy in Britain. On 7 January 1906 a protest meeting presided over by Lord Rothschild at the Queen's Hall condemned the outrages on the Jews in Russia. The meeting was attended by many prominent personages, including the Archbishop of Westminster, and letters of support were received from the Prime Minister and the Archbishop of Canterbury.[30] The anniversary of Bloody Sunday was marked by a number of meetings in which, as a year previously, the S.D.F., the I.L.P., and the Society of Friends of Russian Freedom were particularly active. At a meeting in the Memorial Hall, Farringdon Street, the S.D.F. leader, Hyndman, read a letter from Gorky,[31] and at the Queen's Theatre, Manchester, a meeting was held presided over by Mrs. Pankhurst.[32] There were similar gatherings in other towns. But there was no longer the spontaneous and widespread indignation which Bloody Sunday itself had provoked, and the suppression of the Moscow rising by the army aroused nothing like the same response.

---

[26] See Chernyak, op. cit. (n. 1).

[27] *Justice*, 9 Dec. 1905, p. 4; 16 Dec. 1905, p. 3.

[28] Adams, op. cit. (n. 1), 182.

[29] *Justice*, 24 Feb. 1906, p. 6. See also L. I. Zubok, ed., *Istoriya vtorogo internatsionala* (M., 1966), ii, 146.

[30] *The Times Weekly Edition*, 12 Jan. 1906, p. iv.

[31] *Justice*, 27 Jan. 1906, p. 4.

[32] *The Labour Leader*, 2 Feb. 1906, p. 528.

Meanwhile, Witte was emerging from the pages of the British press as an enigmatic, self-contradictory figure, on the one hand doing what British instincts felt to be necessary, and on the other arousing suspicion because of the Kadets' refusal to join his cabinet and continued denunciation of him. He was thus depicted as vacillating between reform and reaction,[33] and very little thought was given to the difficulties of his position once the October Manifesto had been declared unacceptable by the reformers themselves. It was generally held in Britain that 'the reactionaries' were in control[34] and proof of reaction was seen in the *ukaz* of 11/24 December 1905 on the franchise for the State Duma,[35] and in *ukazes* of 20 February/5 March 1906, which Russian liberal papers, with the apparent approval of *The Times* correspondent, described as a mockery of a constitution.[36] Meanwhile, much interest was roused by reports in *The Times* and the *Tribune* of atrocities in Russian prisons, especially the case of Mar'ya Spiridonova, which led even the sober *Westminster Gazette* to head its summaries of Russian news with 'Reaction in Russia', 'Fiendish cruelty in Russia'.[37] It was now feared that if the Duma actually did meet, it would be immediately prorogued till the autumn. *The Times*, on 2 March, expressed the view that the Duma was only being called so that the government could secure the international loan it needed to maintain itself in power.

The picture of Russia which the British investor now had could hardly persuade him to subsidize the Russian government.[38] Not only were there doubts as to the legality of concluding a loan before the Duma assembled, but there was also the feeling that tsarism would be overthrown and the triumphant reformers might repudiate the debt. *The Economist* consistently advised the British public to avoid the risks of investing in Russia.[39] And so, in March, Noetzlin, director of the Banque de Paris et des Pays-Bas warned Kokovtsov, the Russian negotiator, that Lord Revelstoke, who represented Baring Brothers, was pessimistic about British participation in the proposed loan. In order to help matters forward, arrangements were made by the Russian authorities to bribe the French press. Deborin claims that Witte bribed the British press too.[40] If this is true, it seems to have been a waste of

---

[33] See, for example, the *Daily Graphic*, 14 Nov. 1905, also *Spectator*, 16 Dec. 1905, p. 1027.

[34] *The Times Weekly Edition*, 15 Dec. 1905, p. 787.

[35] *Manchester Guardian*, 29 Dec. 1905.

[36] *The Times*, 8 Mar. 1906.

[37] These reports originated with David Soskice. The author is grateful for confirmation of this fact to Dr. B. Hollingsworth. See R. Reynolds, *My Russian Year* (1913), 191.

[38] This was recognized in a report of Kokovtsov of 11 January—see B. A. Romanov, ed., *Russkie finansy i evropeiskaya birzha v 1904–1906 gg.* (M.–L., 1926), 154 ff.

[39] *The Economist*, 10 Feb. 1906, p. 216; 17 Mar., pp. 442–3; 31 Mar., pp. 533–4. On the other hand the *Board of Trade Journal* consistently depicted Russia as a most suitable field for British enterprise and investment.

[40] G. A. Deborin, *Mezhdunarodnye otnosheniya v period russko-yaponskoi voiny i pervoi russkoi*

money, though arguments in favour of the loan were put forward by Dillon in the *Contemporary Review*: to counteract the German menace Russia must be restored to power in Europe, and for that she needed money; besides, the reforms which British opinion demanded also required funds. The value of Russian support had been illustrated in the help she gave to France at the recent Algeciras conference on Morocco, and participation in a loan would improve British relations with Russia.[41] The loan agreement was signed on 16 April, but the British share was only 330 millions of the total 2,250 million francs.

When the British press altered its focus to consider the international scene in connection with the Algeciras conference, thoughts returned to the possibility of an entente with Russia. As *The Times* put it on 2 April, 'Not a few Englishmen will hope that the Algeciras conference will give a further stimulus to the policy already initiated by Lord Lansdowne and Sir Charles Hardinge, the policy of supplementing the Franco-Russian Alliance and the Anglo-French entente by their natural complement, a cordial understanding between Great Britain and Russia.' Nevertheless, the Foreign Office was conscious that the task of improving relations with Russia was still complicated by the hostility of British public opinion. Recalling the atmosphere of the time, the newly-appointed British ambassador to St. Petersburg, Sir Arthur Nicolson, wrote: 'Among the official classes there existed the old antipathy to Russia. . . . In large sections Russia was regarded as a ruthless and barbarous autocratic state, denying all liberties to her subjects and employing the most cruel methods of suppression of freedom of speech and indeed of thought.' On the Russian side there was a corresponding antipathy which arose partly out of the annoyance caused by constant criticism of Russia in the British press. For these reasons Nicolson believed that discussions should be limited to a matter-of-fact treatment of British and Russian interests in certain specific regions. There could be no thought of a wide understanding.[42]

When Nicolson arrived in St. Petersburg he quickly formed an unfavourable view of the work of British journalists there, as they spoke only of murder, arson, and pillage. In truth, the British public had not

revolyutsii 1904–1907 gg. (M., 1941), 58. J. A. Spender, editor of the *Westminster Gazette* at the time, claims that the British press was above suspicion in this respect, although attempts by foreign interests to bribe it were made (J. A. Spender, *The Public Life* (1925), ii, 133). On the subject of the loan see B. A. Romanov, op. cit. (n. 38), 253 ff.; Olga Crisp, 'The Russian Liberals and the Anglo-French Loan to Russia', *Slavonic and East European Review*, xxxix (1961), 497–511; V. N. Kokovtsov, *Iz moego proshlogo: vospominaniya, 1903–1919* (Paris, 1933), i, 147 ff.

[41] *Contemporary Review*, April 1906, pp. 576–600. Dillon acted as intermediary between Witte and the British government. In January he called on Spring-Rice and broached the subject of a loan, see G. P. Gooch and H. Temperley, eds., *British Documents on the Origins of the War*, iv (1929), 219.

[42] Harold Nicolson, *Sir Arthur Nicolson, bart., First Lord Carnock* (1930), 206; also (Sir Edward) Grey of Fallodon, *Twenty-five Years* (1925), i, 154.

been given an unbiased account of the policies of the various political factions in Russia or a thoughtful examination of the new constitution and the powers of the State Duma. In the nature of things, journalists had tended to concentrate on sensational happenings.

British opinion of Russia was now, in the spring of 1906, in a confused state. Whilst most Britons felt that a compromise between Witte and the liberals should have been possible, the Kadets, who had rejected compromise, were held up as the most able and statesmanlike of all political bodies in Russia. The Kadets' resounding electoral victory strengthened this belief in their brilliance and wisdom, but led British opinion to overestimate their authority and reach some false conclusions about the Duma. It was the general view in Britain that, as the *Labour Leader* put it, the Revolution had been 'astonishingly complete' and that 'the Czar must obey'.[43] Unless Nicholas submitted to the people's representatives, tsarism would be swept away completely.

The publication of the Fundamental Laws on 23 April/6 May was criticized in all sections of the British press as an affront to the Duma, although the actual provisions and the electoral law were thought to be democratic enough. The *Standard*, for example, thought 'the present tentative system is worth a fair trial',[44] but there was little confidence that a fair trial would be given. More and more commentators were beginning to realize that a compromise was unlikely. *The Times* on 10 May spoke of the Kadet programme as containing extreme demands, and acknowledged what *Justice* had been saying all along: the Kadets had been brought to prominence by revolutionary forces they did not control, and they must pay the price. The *Daily Express* wrote, 'In the Czar's dominions there is no such thing as political compromise. . . . The Constitutionalists have shown themselves as incapable of grasping the true principles of parliamentary government as the Reactionaries.'[45]

British opinion thus awaited the opening of the 'Duma of the People's Wrath' on 27 April/10 May with a mixture of hope and apprehension, and the self-contradictory press reactions to the Duma's Address[46] replying to the speech from the throne illustrate well the confusion in British minds. The *Daily Graphic*, for example, on 19 May described the Duma's demands as 'almost anarchic proposals', but argued that they were moderate in the Russian context. The *Westminster Gazette*, basing its comments on an article from Nevinson and on *The Times*, concluded that the Duma has 'displayed its fitness in astounding, almost miraculous fashion' in the Address, but nevertheless implied that the Fundamental

[43] *Labour Leader*, 18 May 1906, p. 764.
[44] *Standard*, 11 May 1906.
[45] *Daily Express*, 9 May 1906.
[46] The Address demanded a ministry responsible to the Duma, reform (or perhaps abolition) of the State Council, a broad amnesty, and a land reform based on the expropriation of large estates.

Laws, as they stood, were satisfactory.[47] *The Times* in a leader of 16 May described the Duma's demands as 'wide and sweeping', but, with the exception of expropriation of land, 'for the most part, moderate'. But the *Daily Telegraph* and the *Morning Post*[48] saw clearly that the Address was far from moderate, that it called for a transfer of sovereignty, and so conflict was inevitable.

The self-contradictions of the newspapers often reflected attempts by leader-writers to reconcile their own feelings, recollected in the tranquillity of London, with the impressions of their correspondents caught up in the excitement and bitterness of the political struggle in Russia. The periodical press on the whole avoided this predicament and was rather more critical of the Duma. The *National Review* expected nothing of the Duma,[49] and in the *Contemporary Review* Dillon described its trend as revolutionary, though he accepted the demand for a fully parliamentary regime as 'fair and reasonable'. In the *Fortnightly Review* in June Paul Vinogradoff, in an article 'Russia at the Parting of the Ways', blamed the government for the present situation, but strongly criticized the Kadets, whose 'professions of moderation . . . are chiefly meant to disclaim responsibility for the use of rougher methods and to secure the choice of a favourable time and place for the battle. Their programme, even in its most reduced expression, cannot be accepted by the Czar.' Vinogradoff pointed out that 'when the country condemned the Octobrists at the elections, it declared implicitly in favour of radical programmes and revolutionary methods', for the Union of 17 October was 'the only party which would have attempted to reconcile the claims of reform with national traditions' and would seek a compromise with a strong monarchy.[50] W. T. Stead's *Review of Reviews* believed the Tsar would have to dissolve the Duma and in so doing he would save Professor Milyukov and his Kadet colleagues, because, if their demands were granted, they would soon be denounced as renegades and would have to bear the brunt of revolutionary disappointment.[51] One of the strongest criticisms of the Duma appeared in the *Outlook*, which under the editorship of J. L. Garvin had achieved a position of great influence: 'Unpunctual, passionate, and extreme, exhausting its moral force in paroxysms of orgiastic oratory, beginning negotiation with ultimatums and demanding a more advanced constitution than any in existence, without the least regard to the political value

[47] *Westminster Gazette*, 19 May 1906.

[48] *Daily Telegraph*, 16 May 1906; *Morning Post*, 16 May 1906.

[49] *National Review*, May 1906, pp. 468–81: 'Russia on Rubicon's Banks, by our special commissioner'.

[50] *Fortnightly Review*, 1 June 1906, pp. 1016–25. In an article 'The First Month of the Duma' in the *Independent Review*, July 1906, pp. 48–63, Vinogradoff criticized the Duma and the Kadets, but argued that the only course now open was to form a cabinet of Kadets.

[51] *Review of Reviews*, June 1906, pp. 561–2.

of natural development, the Russian Parliament has opened a purely revolutionary struggle.'[52]

But against this a greater body of opinion in Britain held that the Duma was proving its ability for parliamentary work and the conflict must be resolved by the formation of a government headed by the Kadet president of the Duma, Muromtsev, or by the Octobrist, Shipov.[53] The affinity of the Kadets with British modes of political thought was frequently underlined by references to Kadet speeches by orators like Kovalevsky and Kokoshkin in which British practices were held up as models for Russia to follow. In contrast the government of Goremykin, who had replaced Witte as premier on the eve of the opening of the Duma, appeared as a primitive, alien tyranny.

Just as in November 1905 pogroms and massacres had prevented a calm examination of the Russian political situation, so now, in mid June 1906, attention was distracted by disorders and pogroms, particularly those at Bialystok. Here was the ultimate proof that the tsarist system was incorrigibly evil. Nicholas must now summon to government the Kadets, the last bulwark of the dynasty.[54] In the *Spectator* Bernard Pares praised Milyukov: 'His political insight has seldom been at fault; in the darkest hours he was never taken in by the Witte subterfuge.'[55] The British journalists of the Foreign Press Association in St. Petersburg were still on the side of the Liberation Movement, and it is somewhat ironic in these circumstances that the Russian radicals should have found encouragement in the columns of British newspapers. *Rech'*, the Kadet paper, regularly carried denunciations of Goremykin's government taken from *The Times*[56] and elsewhere without noting that they were based on correspondence inspired in Duma circles in the first place.[57]

On 9/22 July *Rech'* published an article from London by 'Dioneo' (I. V. Shklovsky) saying that the Russian revolution enjoyed the overwhelming support of the British people. This was undoubtedly an exaggeration, but Bialystok had revived much of the old antipathy towards 'official' Russia, and in this climate optimistic speculation about the prospects of an Anglo-Russian rapprochement, which had been common in May, died down. An article in the *Standard* on 19 May, outlining the probable provisions of an agreement on Asian questions had caused

[52] *Outlook*, 19 May 1906, pp. 674–5. But on 23 June (pp. 834–5), the *Outlook* was advocating a Duma ministry as the only means of putting an end to the mounting chaos in the country.
[53] *The Times*, 21 June 1906.   [54] Ibid.
[55] *Spectator*, 11 July 1906, p. 90.
[56] On the other side the conservative *Novoe vremya* was playing the same game and exaggerating British support for the tsarist regime.
[57] Perhaps from the foreign correspondents who haunted the editorial offices of *Rech'*; see I. V. Gessen, *V dvukh vekakh, zhiznennyi otchet* (Arkhiv russkoi revolyutsii, xxii) (Berlin, 1937), 230.

a considerable stir and German diplomats had made urgent inquiries in London and St. Petersburg.[58] In fact, tentative talks were only just beginning and British opinion was ready for nothing more. Amid the gathering gloom over the Duma and in the aftermath of Bialystok a proposed visit by the British fleet to Kronstadt was condemned in the press and had to be postponed. The *Observer* spoke for most British people in a leader of 24 June: 'Desirous as all serious politicians in this country are for a complete understanding with Russia, it is yet obviously impossible for an English Government to indulge in official philandering with a foreign Ministry which plans and executes Jewish massacres with a cynicism Turkey dare not risk and Nero himself might view with envy. The thing simply cannot be.' The *Westminster Gazette* exclaimed: '. . . the doubt deepens whether tolerable government of any kind, even under a representative system, is possible until the whole of the obsolete and rotten machinery of the present regime is cleared away.'[59] The efforts of the diplomats could hardly be helped by such words from the paper commonly held to be the mouthpiece of the Foreign Secretary, Sir Edward Grey, or by the famous outburst of Campbell-Bannerman, the British Prime Minister, 'La Douma est morte, vive la Douma!'.

The dissolution of the first Duma was universally condemned in Britain, though some commentators felt that the Tsar had merely acted unwisely. There were too some criticisms of the Duma for seeking greater powers than those possessed by the House of Commons or the American Congress.[60] The majority opinion, however, was that the Tsar's action was a deed of perfidy, that 'with the proceeds of the last loan safe in the vaults of the Imperial Bank, the Tsar and his misguided counsellors are under no compulsion to listen to foreign expostulations'.[61] It was confidently anticipated that a great revolutionary upheaval would ensue. The *Manchester Guardian* doubted whether a greater mistake had ever been made by any government.[62] The *Daily Chronicle* foretold another general strike, 'and to its horrors new and more terrible features will be added'. The *Daily News* on 20 July prophesied 'Götterdämmerung, the Twilight of the Gods. The result will not be so much revolution as a kind of cosmic anarchy.' Such fears again gave birth to the spectre of German intervention and European war.

But the dissolution of the first Duma was not followed by the cosmic upheavals which commentators had prophesied. The Russian people

[58] Gooch and Temperley, op. cit. (n. 41), iv, 231; *Die grosse Politik der europäischen Kabinette*, Bd. 25, i (Berlin, 1927), 11 ff. and 202 ff.

[59] *Westminster Gazette*, 24 July 1906. Although the *Westminster Gazette* was believed abroad to be the organ of Sir Edward Grey, the editor J. A. Spender denies that Grey, who was his friend, ever tried to influence his paper. See Spender, op. cit. (n. 40), ii, 131.

[60] *Daily Telegraph*, 24 July 1906. [61] *Daily Graphic*, 24 July 1906.
[62] *Manchester Guardian*, 23 July 1906.

did not rise up to avenge the popular assembly, and they ignored the Vyborg Manifesto issued by the Duma deputies calling for a refusal to pay taxes or provide recruits for the Tsar's army. As the expected revolt failed to materialize, people in Britain began to question their former assumptions about the Duma, or, as Pares complained,[63] lost interest altogether. Whilst it was at first assumed that under the new premier, Stolypin, reaction would reign, and that the second Duma would probably never meet,[64] criticisms of the tactics and policies of parties in the first Duma were becoming ever more frequent. A swing of British sympathies away from Russian radicals and revolutionaries was imminent.

An important role in this was played by Sir Donald Mackenzie Wallace who had come to St. Petersburg in July at the invitation of Sir Arthur Nicolson and with a commission from King Edward to make a thorough investigation of the political situation in Russia. Wallace was to use his influence to persuade the British press, in particular *The Times*, to comment less unfavourably on Russian events.[65] On 11 August *The Times* began publication of a series of articles under the title 'Russia revisited' from 'an Occasional Correspondent', who was suspected of being none other than Wallace himself, but was in fact Dr. Alexander Francis,[66] at one time pastor of the British and American Church at St. Petersburg, respected in Russian official circles, and known to Nicholas II himself. The first article, written from St. Petersburg on 1 August, contained an attack on the Kadets for making common cause with the extremists in the hope of climbing into power by their aid, whilst another article from Peterhof on 10 August examined the Tsar's views and position since October.[67] He had never wavered, we are told, in his determination to institute and keep the Duma in being as an institution, but believed he must appoint the cabinet himself until the Duma found its feet. Once the Centre had allied itself with the Left, Nicholas had decided this Duma must be dissolved. Francis's view was that if the Kadets had united with the Octobrists a great advance in parliamentary government might have been achieved.

[63] B. Pares, *Russia and Reform* (1907), 566.

[64] *The Times*, 23 July 1906.

[65] *History of The Times*, iii, 489. See also W. Harrison, 'Mackenzie Wallace's View of the Russian Revolution of 1905–1907', *Oxford Slavonic Papers*, N.S. iv (1971), 73–82.

[66] The author is grateful for this and much other information to the former curator of the *Times* archives, Mr. W. R. A. Easthope and the present Archivist, Mr. J. G. Phillips.

[67] *The Times*, 18 Aug. 1906. Wallace had an audience with the Tsar at Peterhof on 24 July/ 6 August (*Das Tagebuch des letzten Zaren* (Berlin, 1923), 302), and it was thought that Wallace was the author, or at least the inspirer, of 'Russia revisited'. In a letter to Wickham Steed of 16 August 1906, in the *Times* archives, Wallace denies that he wrote them. On 8 November 1906, in a letter to Lord Knollys, private secretary to King Edward VII, Wallace repeated his denial, but said that the Empress still believed him to be the author of 'Russia revisited'. Photocopies of Wallace's letters to Knollys have been deposited in the *Times* archives, and we quote from them with the gracious permission of Her Majesty the Queen.

At this juncture, on 12/25 August, an attempt was made on the life of Stolypin. During the life of the first Duma the refusal of the Kadets and other major factions to condemn terrorism had been ignored in Britain, where the press had in the main taken the view that terrorism in Russia was not only understandable, but justified. There were some misgivings about this, and G. B. Shaw, for example, himself no lover of tsarism, complained that in supporting any attack on the Russian state *The Times* and other Conservative papers condoned bomb-throwing, and the Madrid assassin, who had made an attempt on the life of King Alfonso, may well have felt that he had *The Times* behind him.[68] The bomb blast at Stolypin's *dacha* on Aptekarsky Island killed more than thirty people and injured more than twenty, including his son and daughter. Although worse things had happened in Russia in the last year or so, news of this deed was met with horror in Britain. *The Times* was right when it said, on 27 August, that the outrage would 'probably alienate more people not only from the revolutionaries, but from the reformers, than any single incident of late in Russia'. Not only were the Russian revolutionaries and their liberal allies discredited in British eyes, so too were the commentators who had supported them. On 26 August the *Observer* wrote, 'Once more prophets and critics will be tempted to discuss Russia, to fathom the unfathomable, and predict the unknowable.' It had at last been brought home to British observers that Russia was in the grip of forces of upheaval that they did not comprehend, and that the alternative to tsarism might be something very different from British-style constitutional government. The average Briton now suspended moral judgement, and the general move to the Right in Russian opinion which led to such phenomena as *Vekhi* was paralleled by a similar shift in British opinion. Bernard Pares, for example, who had been an ardent admirer of the Kadets, transferred his sympathies to Stolypin.[69]

Despite the harsh measures, including trial by field courts martial, with which he responded to the terrorists, Stolypin had a much more favourable press in Britain than Witte. Dillon had doubts as to whether he had the stature to cope with the situation, but described him as 'a Liberal Progressist whose honesty is above criticism',[70] which was the general British view of him. In the autumn of 1906 there began to assert itself a more favourable and optimistic view that Russia, under Stolypin, might after all settle down to develop a liberal constitutional regime. The last article of 'Russia revisited' in *The Times* (18 October) foresaw a stormy second Duma after which recovery would set in: the peasants would be won over to a progressive movement led by the

[68] *The Times Weekly Edition*, 6 July 1906, p. ii.
[69] G. R. Noyes on Bernard Pares, *Slavonic and East European Review*, xxviii (1949–50), 32–5.
[70] *Contemporary Review*, Sept. 1906, p. 444.

Kadets and Octobrists. There were reports that the Kadets had repudiated the Vyborg Manifesto and were adopting a more moderate position, that amicable relations had been established between Stolypin and A. I. Guchkov, the Octobrist leader, and with Count Heyden and other representatives of the Party of Peaceful Regeneration.[71] The *Times* correspondent in St. Petersburg now regarded the outlook as reassuring, and attributed the improvement to the fact that 'for the first time in her history Russia has been governed by men who have sincerely and honestly endeavoured to discharge their duties'.[72] The more favourable tone of the British press was noted by Benckendorf in a letter from London on 11 October, in which he wrote that, whilst it was natural for British sympathies to be on the side of liberal reform, as a result of anarchistic acts British attitudes had recently become more understanding. Stolypin, Benckendorf reported, was popular in Britain, and although some radical papers such as the *Daily News* and the *Tribune* (which Benckendorf called his *bête noire*) went on attacking the Russian government, such attacks were becoming less frequent.[73]

Benckendorf's dispatch had been prompted by the proposal to send a deputation to present an Address from the British public to Muromtsev, president of the first Duma. This project had originated before the demise of the first Duma, the prime mover being the *Tribune*.[74] G. H. Perris records that in August 1906 there was formed in St. Petersburg an Anglo-Russian Friendship Committee for the Promotion of a Rapprochement between the Peoples of Great Britain and Russia, members of which were Muromtsev, Milyukov, and David Soskice. A British committee and a Russian committee were formed to make arrangements for the British delegation to visit Russia. The Address was signed by George Meredith, Thomas Hardy, Rider Haggard, nearly half the House of Commons, many peers, bishops, mayors, professors, artists, and officials of more than 150 trade unions. Amongst representatives of the press were some prominent editors: Robert Donald of the *Daily Chronicle*, J. L. le Breton Hammond of the *Speaker*, W. Hill of the *Tribune*, Hector Macpherson of the *Edinburgh Evening News*, and C. P. Scott of the *Manchester Guardian*.[75] Vast preparations were made in St. Petersburg for the delegation's visit, but with the Duma now dissolved the matter took on the aspect of interference in Russia's internal affairs, and as such was resented by some sections of Russian opinion.[76] King

[71] *The Times Weekly Edition*, 12 Oct. 1906, p. 644; 19 Oct., p. 660; 26 Oct., p. 675.

[72] *The Times*, 1 Nov. 1906.

[73] *Krasnyi arkhiv*, ii (9) (1925), 54–5; and *Au Service de la Russie. Alexandre Iswolsky: Correspondance diplomatique, 1906–1911* (Paris, 1937–9), i, 369.

[74] *Speaker*, 7 July 1906, p. 306; Grey, op. cit. (n. 42), i, 156; letter from Wallace to Knollys, 10 Oct. 1906.

[75] G. H. Perris, *Our Foreign Policy and Sir Edward Grey's Failure* (1912), 98 ff.; *Daily News*, 24 July 1906.

[76] *The Times*, 10 Oct. 1906.

Edward asked Grey to disavow the deputation, but Grey's view was that this would imply disapproval of the Address, which was not in itself objectionable, though the time and manner of its presentation were wrong.[77] Some signatories, including St. Loe Strachey, editor of the *Spectator*, withdrew their support, and the bulk of British opinion was uneasy about sending a delegation in these changed circumstances. In the end it was decided that instead of the delegation, which was to have included Sir George Scott Robertson, Pethick-Lawrence and H. N. Brailsford, the Address would be taken secretly to St. Petersburg by H. W. Nevinson.[78] There was general relief when the plans for a deputation were abandoned. On 19 October, for example, the *Labour Leader* wrote, 'We frankly confess that from the outset we felt dubious as to the wisdom of a British political demonstration on Russian ground in favour of the Russian revolution.'

The struggle for influence over British public opinion thus went on into the autumn of 1906. Milyukov arrived in England and was entertained at the Trocadero on 11 September at a dinner presided over by A. G. Gardiner of the *Daily News*, and at the end of his speech Milyukov raised his glass in honour of British public opinion.[79] Milyukov spoke at other meetings, as did Alad'in. The S.D.F. was again energetic in striving to maintain flagging British sympathy for the revolution in Russia, and *Justice* devoted more space to Russian events as most other papers lost interest. Efforts to raise funds for the revolutionary cause continued. On a motion of Ben Tillett, the T.U.C. agreed to send a circular to affiliated unions asking for financial help for the Russian people in their struggle.[80] An appeal from the British International Committee was signed by Arthur Henderson, Keir Hardie, Hyndman, J. F. Green (of the Society of Friends of Russian Freedom) and others.[81] The *Daily Chronicle*, the *Daily Graphic*, the *Daily News*, the *Manchester Guardian*, and the *Tribune* maintained criticism of the Russian authorities. In *The Times* in October, Lucien Wolf again posed the question 'Is Russia solvent?', and took just as serious a view of Russia's finances as he had in 1905.[82]

Nevertheless, as British opinion cooled towards the revolution, the idea of an entente with Russia became increasingly acceptable, and discussion of the subject began to grow again in the British press, often with hints that Britain might help Russia over the question of the Straits;[83] and amid such speculation the negotiations on a convention

[77] Letter from Grey to Campbell-Bannerman, British Museum, MS. 41218, ff. 87–9.

[78] Nevinson, op. cit. (n. 13), 207–8.

[79] Ibid.; see also *The Times Weekly Edition*, 14 Sept. 1906, p. ii.

[80] *Justice*, 8 Sept. 1906, p. 1; 15 Sept., pp. 1, 3; *The Times Weekly Edition*, 7 Sept. 1906, p. 573.

[81] *Justice*, 19 Jan. 1907, p. 9.   [82] *The Times*, 6 Oct. 1906.

[83] e.g. *Daily Telegraph*, 29 Sept. 1906; Dillon in the *Contemporary Review*, Nov. 1906, pp. 723–46; ibid., Edwin Pears, Feb. 1907, pp. 153–72; *Manchester Guardian*, 19, 22 Jan. 1907. Dillon's disclosures caused some annoyance in St. Petersburg (E. Rozental', *Diplomaticheskaya istoriya*

began to pick up speed. Meanwhile, *The Times* and the Russian authorities settled their differences, and Wilton's position as correspondent was regularized.[84] Commenting on the new situation a leading article on 17 December declared, 'History has cast upon England and Russia the duty and the privilege of promoting together the peace and progress of the Middle East . . .'. Every effort should be made to prevent distrust from poisoning amicable relations. 'To prevent the growth of that mistrust, which many persons are eager to foster, should be the object alike of good Englishmen and of good Russians who have intelligence and knowledge enough to keep steadily in view the historic mission that is shared by their two countries.' From now on *The Times* was to present a more favourable picture of Russia, condemning the excesses of 'the terrorists' where formerly it had berated 'the reactionaries'.

Meanwhile, the famine in Russia gave the British public the opportunity to show that if it was losing interest in the revolution, its sympathy for the Russian people remained undiminished. Appeals from the Zemstvo Relief Association were published in British papers, and many organizations and firms undertook the collection of funds. By early April Prince L'vov was reporting that the *zemstva* had received more than £100,000 from British sources.[85] On 24 March a Russian squadron arrived at Portsmouth and 18 officers and 100 men were taken on a visit to London where a gala performance, attended by Sir Edward Grey and Admiral Sir John Fisher, was held in their honour at the Alhambra. *The Times* recorded on 27 March that the sailors were given an enthusiastic reception by a packed house. The *Daily Express*, in a leader entitled 'John and Ivan', on the same day remarked, 'The hearty cheers which greeted the men of the Russian fleet in the streets of London yesterday prove, at least, that Russophobia is dead.' British attitudes had undergone a considerable change since the Dogger Bank incident. By contrast the Russian Social Democrats who arrived in May to hold their congress in London had a cool reception. *The Times* correspondent wondered about the advisability of countenancing on British soil the congress of people who intended to buy arms for an uprising.[86] *Justice* complained that Scotland Yard was compiling lists of the participants for the tsarist authorities,[87] and the *Labour Leader* expressed the hope that British papers would not publish their photographs.[88] But the *Newcastle Daily Journal*, 20 May, thought they were hardly interesting enough to be photographed. Nevertheless, an enthusiastic reception for them was arranged by the S.D.F. at Holborn Town Hall on 24 May.

russko-frantsuzskogo soyuza (M., 1960), 249, 256). But some of Dillon's dispatches were 'inspired' by the Russian Ministry of Foreign Affairs (A. Iswolsky, op. cit. (n. 73), i, 415).

[84] *History of The Times*, iii, 490 ff.

[85] *The Times Weekly Edition*, 8 Feb. 1907, p. 84; 22 Feb., p. i; 12 April, p. 228.

[86] *The Times*, 13 May 1907.   [87] *Justice*, 1 June 1907, pp. 1, 7.

[88] *Labour Leader*, 24 May 1907, p. 838.

The second Duma, which convened on 20 February/5 March 1907, attracted less attention in Britain and fewer hopes than the first. Most national papers spoke favourably of Stolypin's programme and thought he deserved the support of Russian liberals, but from the outset there were doubts as to whether this Duma would last long. The *Daily Graphic*, *Daily Chronicle*, *Daily News*, *Tribune*, and *Manchester Guardian* remained critical of the Russian government and, in particular, censured Stolypin for not withdrawing the field courts martial. This issue did in fact check the growth of pro-Russian sentiment in Britain for a while.

But British opinion was prepared for the dissolution of the second Duma well in advance, and in this the issue of terrorism was important. On 15 April, for example, *The Times* published a letter from Professor Martens arguing that it would be necessary to dissolve the Duma and enact a new electoral law, though a leader of the same date declared that these steps 'could not be followed without severely shaking the confidence and checking the sympathy with which the friends of Russia in this country and all those who are interested in the political and financial regeneration of the Great Empire have hitherto watched M. Stolypin's wiser and more patient policy'. Harold Williams writing for the *Spectator* had also prophesied an early dissolution and a new franchise,[89] and Pares focussed attention on terrorism. In an article 'The Russian Duma and Political Assassination' Pares came out with criticism of Milyukov for not clearly dissociating himself and his party from terrorism,[90] and in the *Westminster Gazette* on 21 and 23 May he again asserted that the Kadets must break with 'methods which are indeed incompatible with all Parliamentary work'. *The Times* on 21 May also condemned terrorism in Russia and reported Russian criticisms of the Kadets for their failure to condemn terrorist acts. At this juncture, when the British papers were talking of the Social Democrats' efforts to secure arms in Britain,[91] Stolypin claimed to have proof of a Social Democrat plot to stir up mutiny in the armed forces, and over this issue the Duma was dissolved on 3/16 June.

Compared with the outcry which followed the end of the first Duma, British reactions to the second dissolution were divided and muted. The *Daily Telegraph*, 18 June, exulted that Dillon's prophecies had been fulfilled, and the *Daily Express*, 17 June, thought the whole affair showed Russia was not ready for a constitution. The *Daily Mail* did not seem to care. The rest of the papers were in varying degrees critical of the Tsar's action, the general opinion being that the Duma had been dissolved

[89] H. Williams, 'Parties and Tactics in the new Duma', *Spectator*, 23 Feb. 1907, pp. 284–5.
[90] *Spectator*, 20 Apr. 1907, pp. 612–13.
[91] Throughout the 1905 Revolution, British sympathizers had been helping Russian revolutionaries to procure weapons; see M. Futrell, *Northern Underground: Episodes of Russian Revolutionary Transport and Communications through Scandinavia and Finland, 1863–1917* (1963).

on a trumped-up charge. Criticism was restrained in *The Times*, *Westminster Gazette*, *Pall Mall Gazette*, and *Morning Post*. The other papers were more outspoken, the *Standard*, 17 June, even remarking that 'the Czar's unstable mind has suddenly been perverted', whilst the *Manchester Guardian* thought Stolypin had wanted to preserve the Duma, but the Tsar had killed constitutionalism in Russia.[92] The periodical press made little comment and adopted a wait-and-see attitude. In the *Contemporary Review* Dillon was fairly confident that the third Duma would have a moderate majority and would prove a capable legislative body.[93] Pares in the *Spectator* was less hopeful and did not believe the third Duma would be able to exercise authority or help to pacify the country.[94]

The dissolution of the second Duma gave a fillip to protests against an Anglo-Russian understanding. On 18 June, J. A. Hobson presided at a meeting at the South Place Institute where Cunninghame Graham moved a resolution, seconded by Aylmer Maude, protesting against the establishment of friendly relations with the Russian government because it was at war with its own people.[95] The S.D.F., the I.L.P., and the Society of Friends of Russian Freedom organized a joint demonstration on 14 July in Trafalgar Square. A number of arrests were made and this, together with the proceedings against some comrades in other cities on charges of storing explosives intended for Russia led to accusations that the Foreign Office and Scotland Yard were acting in league with the tsarist government. *Justice* reported meetings protesting against an Anglo-Russian entente in Liverpool, Bristol, and Coventry.[96] The National Council of the I.L.P. passed a resolution strongly opposing any move towards an agreement or treaty with the Russian government.[97]

The arguments of the protesters, of course, were that the nature of the tsarist regime was such that any agreement with it was abhorrent. But even for those who had no love for tsarism, there were arguments in favour of an agreement with Russia. An understanding should, after all, relieve Britain of the need to increase her army in India, and British radicals could hardly object to a move which would curtail military expenditure. Moreover, the alternative to an agreement was presumably armed conflict between Britain and Russia.[98] The belief that an entente would strengthen tsarism to the detriment of the reform movement was also challenged. The *Nation* pointed out, furthermore, that the Russian liberals themselves were divided on this question and

[92] *Manchester Guardian*, 17, 19 June 1907.
[93] *Contemporary Review*, July 1907, pp. 116–40; also Dillon in the *Spectator*, 24 Aug. 1907, pp. 257–8.
[94] 'What next in Russia?', *Spectator*, 6 July 1907, pp. 13–14; and 'The Issues in Russia', *Spectator*, 16 Nov. 1907, pp. 768–9.
[95] *The Times Weekly Edition*, 21 June 1907, p. 392.
[96] *Justice*, 6 July 1907, p. 2; 20 July, pp. 1, 6.
[97] *Labour Leader*, 12 July 1907, p. 41.
[98] *Justice*, 24 Aug. 1907, p. 3; *Westminster Gazette*, 18 July 1907.

that possibly a majority thought that closer relations with Britain would allow a greater liberal influence to penetrate into Russia; and some liberals feared that if Russia did not join with Britain, she would move closer to Germany, which would not help the progressive cause in Russia.[99]

By the late summer of 1907 British opinion was in the main well disposed towards an agreement of some kind with Russia, though it had not reached a position at which more than a cautious beginning to an entente was possible. Replying to questions in the House of Commons, Sir Edward Grey insisted that an alliance was not contemplated; the Foreign Office could only negotiate to remove possible causes of quarrel, but friendship with Russia must depend on public opinion.[100]

The Anglo-Russian Convention on Persia, Afghanistan, and Tibet was signed on 31 August. It was denounced by the liberal *Daily News* and the socialist papers *Justice* and the *Labour Leader*, which to the end opposed a deal with tsarism on moral grounds; and there were numerous expressions of sympathy for Persia, which had been divided into spheres of influence.[101] There were also criticisms of the Convention on the grounds that certain British interests were being sacrificed.[102] Nevertheless, the Convention was welcomed by most of the British national press. It is true that the *Manchester Guardian*, *Tribune*, and the *Nation* were apprehensive lest the government and Foreign Office should intend to make the Convention the basis of a wider entente, but they accepted the desirability of an agreement on Asian questions.[103] The *Observer*, 1 September, and *Daily Chronicle*, 24 September, were able to separate Russian internal affairs from foreign policy and warmly welcomed the Convention. Most of the other papers were prepared to go further and commented enthusiastically on the prospects for the growth of friendship between Britain and Russia,[104] so much so that the *Anglo-Russian* was obliged to protest against 'the Russian panegyrics beginning to appear in papers which quite recently were distinguished for their bitter attacks upon the Russian system'.[105] Sir Edward Grey had not

[99] *Nation*, 8 June 1907, pp. 552-3. For Russian liberal support for an Anglo-Russian entente see I. V. Bestuzhev, *Bor'ba v Rossii po voprosam vneshnei politiki, 1906–1910* (M., 1961), 127 ff.

[100] *Hansard*, 1 Aug. 1907.

[101] See F. Kazemzadeh, *Russia and Britain in Persia, 1864–1914* (New Haven and London, 1968), 504-5.

[102] A. Vambéry, 'The Anglo-Russian Convention', *The Nineteenth Century and After*, Dec. 1907, pp. 895–904; P. Landon, 'Views on the Anglo-Russian Agreement, I', *Fortnightly Review*, Nov. 1907, pp. 725–33, and A. Hamilton, 'Views on the Anglo-Russian Agreement, II', ibid. pp. 734–43.

[103] *Manchester Guardian*, 2, 26 Sept. 1907; *Tribune*, 2 Sept. 1907; *Nation*, 28 Sept. 1907, pp. 1078–9.

[104] *The Times*, 2 Sept. 1907; *Pall Mall Gazette*, 2 Sept. 1907; *Morning Post*, 2 Sept. 1907; *Daily Express*, 2 Sept. 1907.

[105] *Anglo-Russian*, Nov. 1907, p. 1131; Landon, op. cit. (n. 102), 725, also spoke of 'the chorus of eulogy which it evoked in the Press!'.

ridden roughshod over British public opinion to foist an unwelcome agreement with Russia on an unwilling nation. An agreement on Asian questions which might lead to a wider understanding with Russia was exactly what most of British public opinion wanted at that time.[106] On 25 September the *Daily Chronicle* wrote: 'We believe that it [the Convention] will pave the way for better commercial relations with Russia in Europe, and we look forward to the day when a Russian constitutional Parliament will carry the entente now begun into a bond of friendship!' It was in this spirit that the British public turned from contemplation of the Revolution of 1905–7 to the prospects of the Anglo-Russian entente.

[106] The controversy, of course, was not at an end. The continuing arguments are described by J. A. Murray in his doctoral dissertation 'British policy and opinion on the Anglo-Russian entente' (Duke University, 1957).

Valery Bryusov and the Nature of Art

By T. J. BINYON

THE following article attempts to trace the development of some aspects of Bryusov's views on art from the 1890s to the 1920s. The subject is not one which has received a great deal of attention: there are articles on isolated aspects of Bryusov's thought,[1] but only one full-length study, which treats the writer from a standpoint rather different to that adopted here.[2]

Bryusov's first attempts to formulate an aesthetic date from the mid 1890s and are dominated by the influence of the French symbolist movement. He felt that poetry had taken a completely new direction in the work of writers such as Verlaine, Mallarmé, and Rimbaud. 'Symbolism is a revolution in poetry which is recreating the very bases of art', he wrote.[3]

His first concern was to define the characteristics of the new art. To do so it was necessary to correct a number of misapprehensions. The most serious of these was the view, put forward in France by Brunetière and adopted in Russia by Volynsky, editor and chief critic of the journal *Severnyi vestnik*, that symbolism could be equated with allegory; a symbolist work contained both a direct real meaning and an indirect metaphysical one; Dante and Goethe were as much symbolists as Verlaine and Mallarmé. Bryusov emphatically rejected this view. 'All assertions that Dante was a symbolist are based on a misunderstanding of words', he wrote. 'Before Verlaine symbolism did not exist.'[4] He amplified this statement in an unpublished article of 1896, in which, after proving to his own satisfaction that there was no allegorical content to be found in a number of French symbolist poems, he wrote: 'As so often happens, a new phenomenon took as its name a term which already existed, *but gave it a new meaning*. . . . The critics, when they came across the schools of *symbolists* (in the new sense), tried to find *symbols* (in the old sense) in their works. From this arose the theory of symbolism as a special kind of allegory. Thus this theory owes its conception to a simple *quaternio terminorum*.'[5]

---

[1] The two most important, both of which deal with Bryusov's early writings, are: K. Loks, 'Bryusov — teoretik simvolizma', *Literaturnoe nasledstvo*, 27–8 (1937), 265–75, and D. E. Maksimov, ' "Apologiya simvolizma" Bryusova i ego esteticheskie vzglyady 90-kh godov', *Uchenye zapiski Leningradskogo pedagogicheskogo instituta im. Pokrovskogo*, 1940 no. 4 (ii), 255–69.

[2] A. Schmidt, *Valerij Brjusovs Beitrag zur Literaturtheorie. Aus der Geschichte des russischen Symbolismus* (Munich, 1963).

[3] Maksimov, op. cit. (n. 1), 265.

[4] Letter to P. P. Pertsov, 13. x. 1895, in: *Pis'ma V. Ya. Bryusova k P. P. Pertsovu, 1894–6* (M., 1927), 45.

[5] Maksimov, op. cit. (n. 1), 265.

Bryusov's own definitions of symbolism were borrowed directly from Verlaine and Mallarmé. Symbolism was 'a poetry of nuances, as opposed to the former poetry of colours', he wrote, quoting Verlaine's '... nous voulons la Nuance encor / Pas la Couleur, rien que la Nuance'.[6] 'Mallarmé himself points out that poetry has one aim—to evoke *moods* in the reader', he stated.[7] 'All the statements of the new school can be reduced to one: to refrain from precise, definite images—to force the reader to guess, since the aim of poetry is to awaken the imagination. The whole system of symbolism consists in this', he wrote elsewhere,[8] echoing Mallarmé's words: '*Nommer* un objet, c'est supprimer les trois quarts de la jouissance du poème qui est faite du bonheur de deviner peu à peu; le *suggérer*, voilà le rêve. . . . Il doit y avoir toujours énigme en poésie, et c'est le but de la littérature — il n'y en a pas d'autres — d'*évoquer* les objets.'[9]

The essence of symbolism, therefore, lay in its suggestive, evocative qualities; it was a 'poetry of hints',[10] creating a mood in the mind of the reader. And the language of poetry thus took on a new importance: 'To create a new poetic language, to work out anew the means of poetry —such is the task of symbolism', Bryusov wrote.[11]

But symbolism was more than just a new literary school for him. 'Symbolism, and only symbolism is poetry', he asserted. 'As there is no salvation except within the Orthodox Catholic Church, there is no poetry except within symbolism.'[12] What was true of symbolism would therefore be true of art in general. And it was from his conception of symbolism that Bryusov came now to evolve more general views as to the nature of art.

These emerge from two basic postulates, one concerning the reader, the other the artist. If the aim of symbolism was to suggest, to evoke, to hint, there must be an object to receive these impressions. Neither the artist nor his work could be complete in themselves; their purpose would remain unfulfilled without an audience. 'The centre of gravity has been transferred to the soul of the reader', he wrote.[13] But at the same time art was an intensely subjective activity; it was the revelation of the poet's soul: 'In poetry, in art the first place is occupied by the very personality of the artist! This is the essence—all else is form! The subject and the idea—they are all form!'[14]

---

[6] Loks, op. cit. (n. 1), 268.

[7] Maksimov, op. cit. (n. 1), 262.

[8] D. E. Maksimov, *Poeziya Valeriya Bryusova* (M., 1940), 43.

[9] J. Huret, *Enquête sur l'évolution littéraire* (Paris, 1913), 60–1.

[10] *Russkie simvolisty*. Vyp. ii. *Stikhotvoreniya Darova, Martova, Miropol'skogo, Novicha i dr.* Vstupitel'naya zametka V. Bryusova (M., 1894), 10.

[11] Loks, op. cit. (n. 1), 272.

[12] Letter to P. P. Pertsov, 18. xi. 1895, in: *Pis'ma V. Ya. Bryusova* (n. 4), 48.

[13] Loks, op. cit. (n. 1), 272.

[14] Letter to P. P. Pertsov, 14. iii. 1895, in: *Pis'ma V. Ya. Bryusova* (n. 4), 13.

It followed therefore that the aim of art was to communicate experience from the artist to the reader or observer: 'symbolism has created a new, still untried organ for the transmission of the most secret movements of the soul', Bryusov wrote.[15] In the preface to *Chefs d'œuvre*, his early book of verse, he formulated the idea again in more general terms: 'The pleasure given by a work of art consists in communion [*obshchenie*] with the soul of the artist.'[16]

In 1898 Tolstoy's *What is Art?* appeared. After reading it Bryusov wrote in his diary: 'Tolstoy's ideas are so close to mine that at first I was in despair, and wanted to write a letter to the press, to object, but then I calmed down and contented myself with a letter to Tolstoy himself.'[17] Nevertheless, Tolstoy's work did stimulate Bryusov to produce a general theoretical essay of his own, a thin brochure of thirty pages entitled *O iskusstve*.[18] Three main influences appear to be present in this essay: that conception of art which Bryusov had derived from his analysis of the French symbolists; the metaphysics of Leibniz, whom he was at the time studying at Moscow university; and Tolstoy's ideas in *What is Art?*, of which Bryusov refuted some, but adopted others as his own.

Bryusov begins the work by pointing out that his ideas coincide with Tolstoy's in one respect, in that they both consider art to be a means of communion. But whereas 'Tolstoy would like to limit the sphere of artistic creation, both externally and in content, . . . I seek freedom in art', he writes.[19] He then goes on to develop certain of his earlier views: the task of the artist is 'to reveal his soul to others',[20] by preserving, incarnating in his work the momentary, ephemeral quality of his own unique moods and emotions. It follows therefore that the personality and sincerity of the artist are all-important—a view which leads to the rejection of the 'art for art's sake' aesthetic. Symbolism, though only a stage, and not the final one, in the development of art, has, through its realization of the importance of language in poetry, found a new means of achieving the above aim.

These views are, however, now integrated into a wider philosophical system, the greater part of which Bryusov owes directly to Leibniz. It is from this philosopher that Bryusov takes the metaphysical bases of his essay, expressed in its final section, which bears the title 'Aspirations': that the ultimate reason of things lies in spirit, or God; that God is absolutely perfect; that all men are different, their difference depending

---

[15] Loks, op. cit. (n. 1), 274.

[16] *Chefs d'œuvre* (M., 1895), 7.

[17] *Dnevniki, 1891–1910* (M., 1927), 32.

[18] Bryusov later explained the strange orthography of the title: 'No one other than L. I. Polivanov [his former school teacher] had assured me that the preposition "ob" is used *only before pronouns*'. 'Avtobiografiya, 1890–1910', in: *Russkaya literatura XX veka*. Pod red. S. A. Vengerova, i (M., 1914), 110.

[19] *O iskusstve* (M., 1899), 9.

[20] Ibid. 12.

on the degree to which they embody divine perfection; and that they all strive towards this perfection.

But to these ideas Bryusov adds another, not from Leibniz, but one which flows naturally from his own earlier views on art: that man strives also for union with his fellows, and that art is one of the means through which this union can be achieved. Here of course Bryusov's views follow those of Tolstoy, who writes in *What is Art?*: 'the aim of life is the union of mankind', and 'the task of Christian art is to establish brotherly union among men'.[21]

However, whereas Tolstoy rejects as bad art, or as not art at all, works which do not forward this aim, Bryusov cannot do so, since he wishes to widen the province of art, not to narrow it. He is supported in this aim by another of Leibniz's beliefs—that expressed in the quotation which stands as an epigraph to *O iskusstve*: 'if we could sufficiently understand the order of the universe, we should find that it exceeds all the desires of the wisest men, and that it is impossible to make it better than it is, not only as a whole and in general, but also for ourselves in particular'.[22]

Holding this view, Bryusov is able to reject a number of Tolstoy's positions. Unlike Tolstoy, he believes that art has no obligation to be moral, since in fact there is no real evil. 'A genuinely comprehended evil', he writes, echoing Leibniz, 'is always a step on the endless road to perfection'.[23] Similarly, a work of art need not be generally understood. 'There are artists who are completely alien to some people; these people should not abuse them, but, saying "I do not understand", should pass by, recognizing their own limitations.'[24] Here Bryusov seems to be directly attacking Tolstoy's harsh dismissal of modern literature in *What is Art?*

However, this attitude leaves Bryusov without any criteria for deciding what is art. He surmounts this by an argument beginning with a Leibnizian premise: individuals are unique; each of their emotions is unique. A work of art transmits unique emotions; it must therefore itself be unique. 'The only characteristic of genuine art is its originality . . . the constant characteristic of false art is that it is imitative', he writes.[25] And for this reason he demands sincerity from the artist and calls on him to strive towards self-knowledge.

In *O iskusstve* Bryusov is dealing with a fundamental problem concerning the nature of art: should art be viewed primarily as a means of expression, or of communication? The two laws of human existence which he posits—man's striving towards perfection and his striving towards union with others—are the metaphysical statement of this

[21] Leo Tolstoy, *What is Art? and Essays on Art*. Translated by Aylmer Maude (1930), 265, 288.
[22] Leibniz, *The Monadology and other Philosophical Writings*. Translated with introduction and notes by Robert Latta (Oxford, 1898), 270–1. Bryusov paraphrases Leibniz slightly.
[23] *O iskusstve*, 13.   [24] Ibid. 17–18.   [25] Ibid. 14.

problem. Ultimate perfection would lead to an art that was pure expression; ultimate union to an art that was pure communication.

For Tolstoy, of course, communication is paramount in art. According to him a work is art only if it is infectious; that is, if it communicates feeling. And the more infectious it is, the larger the circle of people it unites, the better it is.

In *O iskusstve* Bryusov is attempting to give both principles equal weight. But his tendency is always to prefer expression to communication. For him not the infectiousness of the work, but the sincerity of the artist, is the criterion of art. A work can be art, he believes, even if it is obscure, even if it has to wait a hundred or a thousand years for a reader. And a work of art can really be appreciated only by another artist. He pursued this view to its logical conclusion when he wrote: 'An ideal poetic work would be such as to be accessible only to its author'.[26] And it was in this direction—towards expression and away from communication—that he moved in the following years.

In this first period of his literary career Bryusov came to hold a number of basic principles on the nature of art and on the task of the artist which were to guide him, with little change, throughout the rest of his life.

Art, he believes, is a human activity of supreme importance; he quotes with approval Mallarmé's words: 'Tout au monde existe pour aboutir à un livre.'[27] It thus follows that art must be autonomous, it cannot be made to serve any external aim. It is this conclusion, it would seem, which leads him to feel that art should be expressive, rather than communicative.

Art and life cannot be divorced, the poet and his work are one. The poet's duty, therefore, is not only to be sincere, but to push self-knowledge to its extreme, ever to seek new areas of experience. In this he must be bound by nothing, for everything can be the subject of art and no moral judgements can be passed upon it. The poet must strive to give expression to each unique, ephemeral moment of life. Art constantly moves forward, as does life: we demand from the artist not only new content, but also new forms, a new approach to language. 'What if I were to try and write a treatise on spectrum analysis in the language of Homer? I would not have enough words and expressions. The same would happen if I were to try and express the sensations of the *fin de siècle* in the language of Pushkin!' Bryusov exclaimed.[28]

Bryusov soon abandoned a number of the positions he had taken up in *O iskusstve*. 'I would change a great deal of it now. Firstly all the Leibnizian ideas. Then all the unconsidered remarks about communion',

[26] Letter to P. P. Pertsov, 14. iii. 1895, in: *Pis'ma V. Ya. Bryusova* (n. 4), 13.
[27] Loks, op. cit. (n. 1), 274.
[28] *Dnevniki* (n. 17), 13.

he wrote in 1902.[29] His new conception of poetry, one which was to remain the basis of his views on art for the rest of his life, was expressed in the short essay 'Istiny', which appeared in 1901.

I have come to the view [he wrote here] that the aim of creation is not communion [obshchenie], but only self-satisfaction [samoudovletvorenie] and self-knowledge [samopostizhenie]. Language was originally not created for communication between people, but for the clarification of one's own thoughts . . . the poet creates in order to clarify to himself his own thoughts and emotions, to make them definite.[30]

The parallel Bryusov draws here between the origin of language and the nature of poetry is not a new one. It was put forward by Wilhelm von Humboldt, whose theories Bryusov had encountered in the works of the philologist Aleksandr Potebnya. In a later article Bryusov acknowledged his indebtedness to Humboldt and Potebnya and restated his own position:

A. Potebnya, continuing the work of W. von Humboldt, called attention to the remarkable parallelism between the creation of language and the creation of the artist. Language, according to W. von Humboldt's conclusion, arose primarily not as a means of communication, but as a means of cognition [poznanie]. Primitive man gave an object a name in order to distinguish it from other objects and in this way to know it. Similarly, the artist, in creating an artistic image, is trying to give a meaning to something, to know something. . . . All art is a special method of cognition.[31]

In 'Istiny' Bryusov's conclusions on the nature of the creative act are preceded by an analysis of thought and of feeling. In each of these he distinguishes certain factors relevant to the process of artistic creation.

He begins by postulating three axioms without which logical thought would be impossible. The first of these is freedom of will: 'It is possible theoretically to assert that every occurrence is conditioned by a preceding one, and that my thought has a cause. . . . If I sincerely, deeply believed that everything I discover through thought is conditioned, caused by centuries of the past, I would not begin to think.'[32]

The second axiom is the belief that thought is a means of attaining truth: 'Why should I begin to think if I know in advance that my final conclusion will be one more error in a long line of similar ones?'[33]

The final axiom is that of 'plurality of principles' [mnozhestvennost'

[29] Letter to P. P. Pertsov, October 1902, in: D. Maksimov, 'Valery Bryusov i "Novyi put'"', Literaturnoe nasledstvo, 27–8 (1937), 286.
[30] 'Istiny', Severnye tsvety na 1901 god, sobrannye knigoizdatel'stvom "Skorpion" (M., 1901), 195–6.
[31] 'Literaturnaya zhizn' Frantsii', Russkaya mysl', 1909 no. 6, p. 167.
[32] 'Istiny' (n. 30), 189.
[33] Ibid. 190.

nachal]: 'Thought, and life in general, emerge from the conjunction of at least two principles. A single principle is non-existence; a single truth is nonsense. There would be no space if left and right did not exist; no morality, if good and evil did not exist.'[34]

Bryusov then goes on to consider the aim of thought and concludes that it is an end in itself, not a means. '*What* one thinks of, to what conclusions one comes, is a secondary matter, only *how* one thinks is important. Are not Spinoza and Leibniz, Spencer and Schopenhauer equally dear to us, although we do not share the final conclusions of their philosophies?'[35]

At the same time the second axiom stated that thought must be considered a means of perceiving truth. The conclusion could only be that there was not one truth, but many: 'One must only realize that all possible philosophies are equally true; one must, having discovered a truth, not be satisfied, but continue to search. Thought is an eternal Ahasuerus, it cannot stop, its path can have no goal, as this goal is the path itself.'[36]

From thought Bryusov turns to feeling. He distinguishes between two types of feeling: the one superficial and external, the other profound and internal. Superficial feelings are those which govern our lives in general; we fear the more profound ones and strive to ignore them. They reveal themselves only occasionally and momentarily, yet they are the expression of our real selves.

Similarly, there are two kinds of poetry. In one superficial feelings are employed to represent life as it seems to be. Such are the plays of Shakespeare, the poems of A. K. Tolstoy, Maikov, and Polonsky. The other kind of poetry expresses the deeper feelings, represents life as it really is, as in the work of Dostoevsky, Tyutchev, and Fet.

If art is considered a method of cognition two further questions arise: what is the object of its cognition, and in what way does this special method of cognition that is art proceed? In his analysis of thought and feeling Bryusov seems to be trying to answer these questions.

In dealing with feeling Bryusov himself points out the connection with art. There are certain feelings which provide us with an intuitive apprehension of things, not as they seem to be, but as they really are. They form the content of what Bryusov terms 'living art', as opposed to 'dead art', the expression of superficial feelings. 'Living art', he writes, 'always "wanders in the abyss", is always in contact with the mysteries—as mystery is its soul, its animating principle.'[37]

Though in 'Istiny' Bryusov does not draw an analogy between his description of the process of thought and the process of creation, the relevance of his remarks in their application to art is clear.

---

[34] 'Istiny', 190.   [35] Ibid.   [36] Ibid. 191.
[37] Letter to P. P. Pertsov, October 1902, in: Maksimov, op. cit. (n. 29), 287.

Art must be autonomous, for there is no final truth for it to serve. Each work of art embodies its own truth, but not to the exclusion of all others. And, following from this, attention must be turned primarily not to what the artist says, but to how he says it: 'Works of art cannot be judged worthy or unworthy according to content, they differ only in form.'[38]

Yet a contradiction arises here, since feeling cannot be considered purely as object, nor thought as method. It follows that the two concepts of art which derive from its comparison with feeling and its comparison with thought are diametrically opposed. To view art as the intuitive apprehension of transcendent values leads, at the extreme, to the belief in the existence of an absolute truth, which all art strives to express. From here it is but a step to considering the aim more important than the means; that is, to denying the autonomy of art. In this conception of art content naturally predominates over form. The other view of art, stemming from the comparison with thought, denies the existence of an absolute truth and emphasizes form over content.

The dichotomy is, in a sense, still that which had confronted Bryusov in *O iskusstve*: between art as communication, as content—seen now as that moment of revelation when two souls 'gaze into each other's depths',[39] and art as pure expression, form. And it is from the tension between these opposing concepts that Bryusov's views on the nature of art arise.

Although Bryusov had now abandoned some of the conclusions of *O iskusstve*, the basic tenet of his former theory, that art is essentially subjective, remained. The personality of the poet took on even greater importance. In a letter to Zinaida Gippius he wrote: 'Unsigned verses simply do not interest me. Verse by itself is neither beautiful nor ugly, it is nothing. It becomes desirable or undesirable only as part of the artist, as instants of his experience, as his life.'[40] Once again he proclaims that life and art are one, that the artist must constantly seek new experience to enrich his work. The criterion of a genuine modern poet is his willingness to use his whole life as his material. Bryusov sees this quality in the poet Ivan Konevskoy, of whom he writes:

What was most astounding about Konevskoy was his eternal, inexhaustible, desperate consciousness of his own actions. . . . He, as it were, did not live, but watched a play in which he was the chief actor, did not act under the influence of passion, but carried out various experiments on his own soul. . . . For him poetry was that which it must be in essence: the clarification for the poet of his own thoughts and emotions.[41]

[38] 'Istiny' (n. 30), 196. [39] Ibid. 195.

[40] Letter to Z. N. Gippius [draft], 1902. Gosudarstvennaya biblioteka SSSR imeni Lenina. Otdel rukopisei, *fond* 386, 70/37.

[41] *Dalekie i blizkie. Stat'i i zametki o russkikh poetakh ot Tyutcheva do nashikh dnei* (M., 1911), 65–6.

A natural corollary to the concept of poetry as a subjective activity, indissolubly linked with the life of the poet himself, was the view that each poet must form for himself a consistent philosophy, an attitude towards life.

> The lyric poet . . . who reproduces in musical lines the impressions he has experienced, must relatively soon come to the fatal limits of his poetry. . . . Only a definite philosophy, which gives a meaning to the passing moments and orders them in the perspective of consciousness, can reveal all their infinite variety.[42]

In his later work Bryusov does not return to the problems he has raised in *O iskusstve* and 'Istiny'; the conclusions he reaches in the latter essay remain the basis of his thought. Henceforward he is concerned more with the particular questions of the content and method of art.

Bryusov's most explicit expression of the concept of art which derives from his analysis of feeling in 'Istiny'—as an intuitive apprehension of the eternal mysteries of life—was contained in a lecture delivered in March 1903 entitled 'Klyuchi tain'. Here, after examining a number of theories on the nature and purpose of art, Bryusov concludes that no rational explanation of art can ever be completely satisfactory. 'The only method which can hope to decide these questions is that of intuition, the inspired guess, a method which has always been used by philosophers and thinkers who sought to resolve the mysteries of existence.'[43] And the answer to the riddle of art given by these methods is one already adumbrated in the philosophy of Schopenhauer:

> Art is the apprehension of the world through other, irrational means. Art is that which in other spheres we call revelation. The creations of art are half-open doors to Eternity.[44]

In the rest of his article Bryusov goes on to develop this idea. The world we perceive with our external feelings is a false one: our sight and hearing deceive us. Reason and science are incapable of revealing the true nature of the world to us. But there are ways of overcoming this ignorance; these are those 'moments of ecstasy, of suprasensible intuition, which give other apprehensions of the appearances of the world and penetrate more deeply beyond their outer shell into their inner substance'.[45] The task of art is to preserve these moments of revelation and inspiration. It follows that art is in essence mysterious, since it deals with the unknowable. Artists have always subconsciously pursued this aim, but it is only now that it has become evident to all. Those who have sought to make art useful have set their sights far too low:

Those questions of existence which art can resolve will never cease to be

42 *Dalekie i blizkie*, 103.
44 Ibid.
43 'Klyuchi tain', *Vesy*, 1904 no. 1, p. 19.
45 Ibid. 20.

important. Art is perhaps the greatest force which mankind possesses. While all the crowbars of science, the axes of social life have not been able to break down the walls and doors which imprison us, art contains a terrible dynamite which will destroy these walls; more than that, it is that sesame which will cause these doors to open of their own accord. Our modern artists should consciously forge their works in the shape of keys to the mysteries, mystic keys, opening for man the doors of his 'blue prison' and leading him forth to eternal freedom.[46]

The ideas put forward in 'Klyuchi tain' are developed in a number of articles of the same period. One of the most interesting, for the light it throws on the dominant erotic themes in Bryusov's verse, is 'Strast'', which appeared in 1904.

Why, Bryusov asks here, do all critics find modern love immoral? The answer lies in the new conception of love it embodies, a conception which, to a certain extent, resembles that held in Ancient Greece and during the Renaissance: the body, the flesh, so long subjugated to the spirit, has regained its rights. This new cult of the flesh, initiated by Nietzsche and the French symbolists, is naturally accompanied by a cult of passion, that moment in which the body finds its fullest expression. In passion we escape from the fetters of mind and will, we experience 'moments of a fullness of sensation in which everything is drowned, ceases to be, and in which the infinity of our true "I" is directly revealed'.[47]

But, Bryusov continues, if, unlike the idealists, we have recognized the importance of the physical, we have also, unlike the materialists, realized that life is not as it appears to be: 'Even recently the world seemed a huge building of solid marble, which it was man's task to examine and measure. . . . Suddenly the "unknowable" opened around us, in everyday life itself. . . . We have only vaguely begun to realize that we are surrounded by mysteries, that we live in a world of mystery'.[48]

Passion, too, unlike love, is a mystery: 'Passion in its essence is a riddle; its roots are beyond the world of man, beyond the earth, beyond us. When passion overcomes us we are near those eternal limits which circumscribe our "blue prison".'[49]

Critics accuse the new art of being not only immoral, but also perverse. But perversity is a meaningless concept, since morality can never be defined absolutely, but only relatively, with reference to accepted convention. And what is immorality? It is not passion itself, but the attitude adopted to it. To be chaste is to recognize the seriousness of passion; to treat it with frivolity is to be immoral. 'Critics, however,'

---

[46] Ibid. 21.
[47] 'Strast'', *Vesy*, 1904 no. 8, p. 23.
[48] Ibid. 24–5.   [49] Ibid. 25.

writes Bryusov, returning to one of the positions taken up in 'Istiny', 'ask only *what* the artist represents, not *how* he represents it'.[50]

Bryusov sees passion, physical love as an epiphany, one of those instants of revelation which it is the purpose of art to embody. In this sense it is, like art, a mystic and religious activity. 'What for the Hellenes was a pleasure has become for us both mystic and sacred', he writes.[51]

In 'Klyuchi tain' and 'Strast'', together with other writings of the same years, Bryusov seems to be approaching those views on art held by the majority of the Russian symbolists, which owe their origin predominantly to the philosophy of Vladimir Solov'ev: that it is a mystical, religious activity, the task of the artist being to reveal the divine essence of reality. However, this view implies a belief in an absolute truth and will ultimately lead to the denial of the autonomy of art. The difference between this position and that of Bryusov emerges clearly in a letter to Zinaida Gippius, written in 1902. Here, discussing an earlier remark she had made, that 'art must become religious', Bryusov writes:

I could even accept this formula, only this would be dishonest, because by *religious* I do not mean the same as you do. You do not distinguish religion from Christianity. For you the beliefs of the Assyrians are interesting only in their relation to Christianity. Not only am I unable even to think in such a way, I cannot even understand how it is possible to *think* like this. In other words, how can one consider one's convictions indisputable, final and essentially true?[52]

Here Bryusov reasserts the other basic principle expressed in 'Istiny', that of the relativity of all truths, and so implicitly affirms the autonomy of art.

In the above letter he points out that in his usage the word 'religious' has very different implications from those it has when Gippius uses it. He makes the same point in another letter of the same year written to P. P. Pertsov, a friend of the Merezhkovskys and editor of the journal *Novyi put'*: '[Art] is always philosophical, mystical, even religious if you like—I am perfectly capable of using this word, although I would give it a different, wider meaning than the one it would have in your speech.'[53]

Indeed, Bryusov often equates art and religion, both in his theoretical writings and his verse. For him the poet is a priest: 'Only the sacerdotal knife, laying open our breast, gives us the right to call ourselves poets', he writes.[54] But this statement is only the expression of the high seriousness of the artist's role; it is not the denial of the freedom of art, not the belief that art should serve religion, but rather the extreme assertion of

[50] 'Strast'', 28.   [51] Ibid. 26.
[52] Letter to Z. N. Gippius [draft], 1902 (n. 40).
[53] Letter to P. P. Pertsov, October 1902, in Maksimov, op. cit. (n. 29), 287.
[54] 'Svyashchennaya zhertva', *Vesy*, 1905 no. 1, p. 29.

its independence. In the same way, terms such as 'mystic' or 'mysteries' do not have the same connotations in Bryusov's work as they tend to have in that of other symbolists. For Bryusov art was the 'key to the mysteries' only inasmuch as it was a search for the unknowable. But his mysticism was never theurgic, as it was in the philosophies of Ivanov and Bely.

The similarity between Bryusov's terminology and that of the other symbolists is confusing and did, moreover, cause him at times to be misunderstood by his contemporaries. In 1910, for example, when he attacked the theurgic view of art held by Ivanov and Blok, Bely, who always suspected him of Machiavellian cynicism, accused him of betraying his former artistic ideals.[55] However, there can be no doubt that Bryusov's thought is essentially consistent; the belief that art is a supremely important activity, an end in itself, which must never be subordinated to any ideology external to it, is one which accompanies him from the beginning to the end of his life as an artist.

In the next few years Bryusov gradually turned away from the views expressed in 'Klyuchi tain'. This was, no doubt, partly due to the fact that these ideas could easily be distorted and wrongly interpreted as a call for art to serve a religious end. More importantly, however, the concept of the work of art as a mystic revelation of the truth, whether relative or absolute, tended to turn symbolism into allegory; the representation of reality in itself lost all importance, since it became only a means for the perception of the transcendental. The second of these developments was as unacceptable to Bryusov as the first.

In the 1890s he had rejected allegory as being incompatible with symbolism. But since then his position had changed. He no longer considered symbolism to be the only possible type of poetry. His dislike of allegory and of the predominance of idealism over realism in poetry were based on other reasons. For him the life and work of a poet were indissolubly connected; the poet must continually seek new experience as material for his art. And by this Bryusov does not mean 'mystic', but 'real' experience: the poet must plumb life, in all its aspects, to the depths. 'The poet always, like Antaeus, gains his strength only *from contact with the earth*', he wrote.[56]

It was thus natural that he should view the growing abstraction of poetry with concern:

We 'decadents', protagonists of the 'new art' [he wrote in 1904] are all in some way isolated from everyday reality, from that which people like to call the real truth of life. We pass through the life which surrounds us, but remain alien to it (and this, of course, is one of our weakest features), as though we

---

[55] V. Ya. Bryusov, 'O "rechi rabskoi", v zashchitu poezii', *Apollon*, 1910 no. 9, pp. 31–4; A. Bely, 'Venok ili venets?', *Apollon*, 1910 no. 11, pp. 1–4.

[56] *Dalekie i blizkie* (n. 41), 177.

were under water in a diving-bell, retaining only telegraphic contact with those who remain beyond this sphere, on the surface, where the sun is shining.[57]

In reaction to this development, Bryusov called for a return to realism in art. 'The artist cannot do more', he wrote, 'than represent reality truly, even if in new, fantastic combinations of its elements. Anyone for whom this is insufficient should leave art and look for something else in science, philosophy, theurgy and the like.'[58] 'The basis of all art', he stated, 'is the observation of reality.'[59]

Linked with the call for a return to reality in art was another: that art should above all be contemporary. This had always been an important principle in Bryusov's thought; for him art and the artist formed the vanguard of the never-ending progress forward that was life. The task of the symbolist poet, he had announced in 1894, was to 'deal with the moods and feelings of contemporary man'.[60]

This view was now reinforced by Bryusov's acquaintance with the ideas of the French poet René Ghil, under whose influence Bryusov's conception of the nature and purpose of art was to take its final form.

Ghil had coined the term 'poésie scientifique' to describe his view of art. This did not mean that poetry should be the mere rephrasing of scientific discoveries, it had a far wider import. 'Ce que Ghil s'est toujours proposé d'exprimer, c'est une émotion qu'il identifie à l'émotion poétique elle-même, et qu'on pourrait dénommer l'émotion cosmique', wrote one of his disciples.[61] Poetry was the expression of existence itself. '[Ghil's] "Œuvre"', wrote Bryusov, 'will embrace the whole universe, in all the forms of its existence—from the cosmic processes to the intricacies of contemporary social life.'[62] 'Le rôle du poète', in Ghil's view, 'est de partir des résultats partiels des sciences pour les ordonner en synthèse et, de là, oser l'hypothèse constructive.'[63]

This view of poetry as something which begins where science ends, of the poet as the bearer of 'l'émotion cosmique', has obvious affinities with the ideas of 'Klyuchi tain'. But Ghil introduces a new element. 'He insists', wrote Bryusov, 'that poetry must take its stand on the heights of contemporary scientific philosophy.'[64]

Bryusov himself had already demanded reality and contemporaneity in art; Ghil's ideas echoed his own and added to them an extra dimension: the importance of the discoveries of modern science to the poet's world.

---

[57] Review of: F. Sologub, *Kniga skazok* (M., 1904), *Vesy*, 1904 no. 11, p. 50.
[58] 'Karl V. Dialog o realizme v iskusstve', *Zolotoe runo*, 1906 no. 4, pp. 66–7.
[59] *Dalekie i blizkie* (n. 41), 145.   [60] *Russkie simvolisty* (n. 10), 8.
[61] René Ghil, *Choix de poèmes* (précédé d'un exposé sommaire des théories du poète et d'un argument détaillé de son œuvre) [G. Brunet, N. Bureau, P. Jamati, eds.] (Paris, 1928), 9–10.
[62] 'Rene Gil', *Vesy*, 1904 no. 12, p. 21.
[63] René Ghil, op. cit. (n. 61), 16.   [64] 'Rene Gil' (n. 62), 18.

It is these elements—the real, the contemporary, the scientific—
which Bryusov henceforth sees as forming the proper content of poetry.
Art is still, as he put it in 'Klyuchi tain', 'perhaps the greatest force
which mankind possesses', but its intuitions now belong to the sphere
of reality, not of mystery. 'For me the transcendental is transcendental,
that is absolutely unknowable. . . . Man's task is to widen the limits of
his consciousness, not to overleap them', he wrote in 1908.[65]

From this point on Bryusov's views on art undergo no real development, but the philosophy he has formed is used to judge—and, in most
cases, to find wanting—contemporary literature. 'Modern poetry is, for
the most part, alien to modern life', he wrote in 1909:

> Man's views of nature and the universe, of good and evil, are changing;
> relations between people are changing; all forms of life are changing; but
> poetry seems not to notice any of this. Poets do not dare to deal with the
> problems that excite modern society, but go on lisping their old songs. . . .
> What is more, despite the noble efforts of a few innovators, such as Baude-
> laire or, in our times, Verhaeren, to introduce into poetry images taken from
> the life we live, the majority of poets up to now have been unable to rid them-
> selves of the accessories of romanticism or antiquity. We live in the world of
> the telegraph, the telephone, the stock-exchange, the theatre, the scientific
> congress, the world of ocean liners and express trains, but poets continue to
> use images which are completely alien to us, which are preserved only in
> verse, images which turn the world of poetry into a dead and conventional-
> ized world.[66]

It was natural that Bryusov, holding such views, should greet the
appearance of the futurist movement with enthusiasm. For him the
most important element in futurism—which he seized on to the exclusion of all others—was its dedication to absolute modernity. 'Of the
tasks put forward by Marinetti's school', he wrote, 'perhaps the most
worthwhile is that of expressing the contemporary spirit.'[67] But futurism
proved a disappointment; it turned in other directions, away from what
he considered the real tasks of poetry. In a later article he expressed his
regret and incomprehension of the futurists' aims:

> Since they [the futurists] live in cities, they should write not of streams,
> fields and oceans, but of our chaotic urban life. The poetry of machines is
> futuristic poetry. I am surprised that the futurists, instead of fulfilling their
> direct purpose, should depict the life of primitive man, or indeed compose
> verse consisting only of vowels and consonants. They—the futurists—have
> a splendid position, but they themselves repudiate it.[68]

---

[65] Letter to E. A. Lyatsky, 12. iii. 1908, in: I. Yampol'sky, 'Iz proshlogo. Neopublikovannye pis'ma V. Bryusova i A. Bloka', *Novyi mir*, 1932 no. 2, p. 194.
[66] 'Literaturnaya zhizn' Frantsii' (n. 31), 160.
[67] 'Novye techeniya v russkoi poezii. Futuristy', *Russkaya mysl'*, 1913 no. 3, p. 128.
[68] 'Zdravogo smysla tartarary. Dialog o futurizme', *Russkaya mysl'*, 1914 no. 3, p. 84.

Bryusov's reaction to the Russian revolution was conditioned by these same views. 'This new world, bathed in the effulgent radiance of to-morrow', as he wrote in 1917,[69] opened up entirely new poetic possibilities. For him its significance as a subject for art in some ways encompassed and transcended its other aspects. 'Poetry is always a reflection of its times', he wrote:

Our years, the epoch after the war and the October revolution, differ in a most profound way from the preceding years: we are living in a new social order, we are creating a new way of life, we are full of new hope, we are setting ourselves new goals; the leadership has been taken over by a new social class which gradually, as opportunity arises, is communicating its ideology to all others. On the one hand the previously impossible is now part of our life; on the other—much that was important and seemed significant in the past is retreating into history, vanishing; finally, language itself, the basic material of poetry, is changing before our eyes. The task of poetry must be to incarnate the experiences of this moment of history, to detect the questions that are being posed, and to give its artistic answer to them.[70]

And as the proletariat was now the dominant class, so it was the 'proletarian' writers who were to assume the task of creating art in the image of the new, transformed society. 'In the final resort "proletarian" poetry is that which should become "poetry" in general', Bryusov stated.[71] However, he found the actual productions of these writers disappointing. If the futurists had abandoned contemporary content, the 'proletarian' poets did not meet the challenge of contemporary form. 'Real proletarian poetry will be the result of a new proletarian culture and will be as different from the poetry of the past as *The Song of Roland* is from the *Aeneid*, or Shakespeare from Dante', Bryusov commented.[72]

Bryusov's post-revolutionary views have often been seen as a betrayal of his former ideals. In fact, his ideals never changed, and his later views are a perfectly consequential development of his thought. There is a certain similarity between Bryusov's view of the task of art and the Marxist conception of the nature of art. Bryusov believes that art should reflect the reality of contemporary society; Marxism tells us that art, as part of the superstructure of society, must reflect the essence of that society: the ideology of its ruling class. There is, however, a vast difference between these two approaches. That art which Bryusov condemned for its failure to come to grips with modern life is, for the Marxist, an illustration of the bankruptcy of the bourgeois ideology that produced it. For Bryusov art is all-important, for the Marxist, ideology.

---

[69] 'O novom russkom gimne', *Vetv'. Sbornik Kluba moskovskikh pisatelei* (M., 1917), 258.
[70] 'Vchera, segodnya i zavtra russkoi poezii', *Pechat' i revolyutsiya*, 1922 no. 7, p. 45.
[71] Ibid. 46.
[72] 'Proletarskaya poeziya', *Khudozhestvennoe slovo*, 1920 no. 1, p. 54.

Indeed for him, from the beginning to the end of his life, art was always the supreme value and the poet always, by virtue of his calling, superior to and different from all other men. 'The poet is neither a philosopher, nor an orator, nor an agitator', he wrote in 1920:

> The poet apprehends all the latest discoveries of science. . . . The poet must equal in knowledge the greatest scientists of his day, must, in depth of thought, yield to no contemporary philosopher, must rival in strength of will the most active revolutionary. . . . The poet, in the intensity of his perception and sensation, is superior to the most subtle organism of his age. A great responsibility rests upon the poet. He is a synthesis of all will, all desire, all emotion. In him each man recognizes himself. The poet is the voice of mankind.[73]

The ideal may be chimerical, but it is worthy of respect. And this is the ideal which sustained Bryusov throughout his literary career; an ideal which found an echo in the thoughts of René Ghil; an ideal expressed, if in very different language, in 'Klyuchi tain': that of the poet as mediator between man and the universe.

[73] B. M. Sivovolov, 'Neopublikovannaya stat'ya V. Bryusova "Ktematika" ', *Nauchnye doklady vysshei shkoly. Filologicheskie nauki*, 1964 no. 3 (27), 188–9.

The Struggle for Power in North-east Russia, 1246–9

An Investigation of the Sources

By J. L. I. FENNELL

IN studying the events of the years immediately following the Mongol invasion of 1238 the historian of north-east Russia is beset by two major difficulties: firstly, there are no major surviving chronicle codices prior to the great *svod* of 1305, which may have undergone editing at the hands of Lavrenty and his assistants some seventy years later;[1] and secondly, most major Russian chronicles of the fourteenth to the sixteenth centuries contain clearly discernible traces of individual princely annals of the thirteenth century in which the events of each reign were recorded from the political standpoint of whoever was grand prince. As the descendants of Vsevolod III succeeded each other to the throne of Vladimir in quick succession in the 1240s and the 1250s and as there was often clearly little love between them, it is not surprising to find that such annals were censored, mutilated, abridged, and often excised by the chroniclers of successive rulers. Thus, a prince who had forcibly removed his brother from the throne of Vladimir would see to it that his predecessor's 'misdeeds' were expunged from the record or turned to redound to his own glory. As a result the surviving chronicles often contain glaring inconsistencies and seemingly inexplicable lacunae. One such lacuna is to be found in the Laurentian Chronicle (abbr. *L*) *s.a.* 1246–9.

The events concerning the occupancy of the grand-princely throne are described in the following sequence:

В лѣто 6754... Тое же осени Ярославъ князь, сынъ Всеволожь, преставися во иноплеменницѣхъ, ида отъ Кановичь, мѣсяца семтебря въ 30 на память святаго Григорья. В лѣто 6755. Слышавъ Олександръ смерть отца своего, приѣха из Новагорода в Володимерь, и плакася по отцѣ своемь с стрыемъ своимъ Святославомъ и с братьею своею. Того же лѣта Святославъ князь сынъ Всеволожь сѣде в Володимери на столѣ отца своего, а сыновци свои посади по городомъ, яко бѣ имъ отець урядилъ Ярославъ. Того же лѣта поѣха Андрѣи князь Ярославичь в Татары к Батыеви, и Олександръ князь поѣха по братѣ же к Батыеви. Батыи же почтивъ ею и посла я г Каневичемъ.

В лѣто 6756... Тое же зимы убьенъ бысть Михаило Ярославичь от поганыя Литвы. Блаженыи же епископъ Кирилъ посла взя тѣло его и

---

[1] See G. M. Prokhorov, 'Kodikologicheskii analiz Lavrent'evskoi letopisi' in: *Vspomogatel'nye istoricheskie distsipliny*, iv (L., 1972), 77–104. Cf. A. N. Nasonov, *Istoriya russkogo letopisaniya XI — nachalo XVIII veka* (M., 1969), 179–81, and Ya. S. Lur'e, 'Troitskaya letopis' i moskovskoe letopisanie XIV v.', in: *Vspomogatel'nye istoricheskie distsipliny*, vi (forthcoming).

привезоша и в Володимерь, и плакашася братья его и боляре над нимъ и пѣвше песни погрѣбалныя и положиша и в стѣнѣ у святое Богородици на память святаго имярекъ. Тое же зимы у Зупцева побѣдиша Литву Суждальскыи князь.

В лѣто 6757... Тое же зимы приѣха Олександръ и Андрѣи от Кановичь, и приказаша Олександрови Кыевъ и всю Русьскую землю, а Андрѣи сѣде в Володимери на столѣ.[2]

It would appear from the above that Svyatoslav Vsevolodovich, who succeeded his brother Yaroslav, remained on the throne of Vladimir for some three years, during which time Yaroslav's two eldest surviving sons, Aleksandr and Andrey, went to and returned from Central Mongolia (*g Kanevichem . . . ot Kanovich'*), while his third son Mikhail was killed fighting the Lithuanians. Eventually in the winter of 1249/50 (*toe zhe zimy* 6757—i.e. before 1 March 1250) Andrey 'sat upon the throne in Vladimir'. Now not only is this account contradicted by other versions, but also it fails to explain what exactly happened to Svyatoslav when Andrey acceded—seemingly peaceably—to the throne. All we learn from *L* and the identical Trinity Chronicle (abbr. *T*) is that in the autumn of 1250 Svyatoslav went to the Horde and that he died on 3 February 1253.

All other chronicles, except for those that derive directly or indirectly from *L* and *T* (such as the Moscow *svod* of 1479, the Ermolinskii Chronicle and Part I of the *Tverskoi sbornik* (abbr. *TS(I)*),[3] throw a different light on the proceedings. There are two quite separate versions. According to the first of these Svyatoslav was ousted from the throne of Vladimir by his nephew Andrey (*prognati* is the verb used); according to the second—by Andrey's brother Mikhail.

The first of these two accounts is found in the oldest dated Russian chronicle fragment, the so-called *Letopisets Nikifora vskore* (abbr. *LN*),[4] which, for all its brevity, is of considerable value as a supplementary source for the history of north-east Russia in the thirteenth century: the Russian entries which follow the Chronicle of the Patriarch Nicephorus go only as far as 1278 and many of them are undoubtedly contemporaneous with the events they describe. The facts relating to Svyatoslav and Andrey are reported laconically:

Ярослав умре въ Татарехъ. По немь сѣде въ Володимѣри Святославъ брат его лѣт[о] 1, и прогна Андрѣи сынъ Ярославль и княжи лѣт 5 и приде Неврюнь от Адама лѣт(о) 6760 и прогна и за море.

[2] *Polnoe sobranie russkikh letopisei* (abbr. *PSRL*), i (M., 1962), col. 471. The account found in the reconstructed Trinity Chronicle is identical. See M. D. Priselkov, *Troitskaya letopis'. Rekonstruktsiya teksta* (M.–L., 1950), 322.

[3] *PSRL*, xxv (M.–L., 1949), xxiii (Spb., 1910) and xv (M., 1965). All of these versions contain the same facts in the same chronological order.

[4] For the text and a brief introductory note, see M. N. Tikhomirov, 'Zabytye i neizvestnye proizvedeniya russkoi pis'mennosti', *Arkheograficheskii ezhegodnik za 1960* (M., 1962), 234–43.

Although this account omits any mention of Andrey's journey to Karakorum it is of value in that, unlike the Laurentian and Trinity Chronicle versions, it tells us what happened to Svyatoslav. As far as the chronology of the entry is concerned it corresponds with that of all other chronicles. We know that Yaroslav died in 1246; consequently, if this account is a true version of what occurred, Svyatoslav must have been driven out by Andrey at the end of 1247, i.e. five years before the latter himself was ousted in 1252. Thus, if we assume that Andrey did in fact journey to Central Mongolia, he must have set off immediately after removing his uncle, for we know that he was certainly in Vladimir before March 1251: according to *L* and *T* Metropolitan Kirill married him to the daughter of Daniil Romanovich 'in the winter' of 6758.[5]

In general, the Russian entries in *LN* are so sparse and fragmentary that it is hard to say which thirteenth-century chronicle *svod* the *letopisets* could have been based on. However, judging from those items which clearly originated in Rostov and from the fact that much of the chronicle is concerned with the history of the grand principality of Vladimir, it would appear that it derived from, and abridged, a Rostov version of the grand-princely chronicle of Vladimir.[6] Many of the chronicle's items, of course, found their way unabridged into the grand-princely *svod* of 1305 (and thence into *L* and *T*). But some did not, and among them the mention of Andrey's forcible removal of Svyatoslav. Yet curiously enough this particular item, which by-passed the *svod* of 1305, managed to trickle through to some later chronicles.

The closest reflection of this fragment of *LN* is to be found in the Novgorod Fourth Chronicle (abbr. *N4*):

В лѣто 6755... А Ярославъ Всево[ло]дичь преставися в кановѣ въ-рдѣ, княживъ въ Володимерѣ лѣто. Святославле. По немь сѣде братъ его Святославъ. Андрѣево. И по единомъ лѣтѣ прогна Андрѣи хоробри торови [var. хоробри татаровѣ], сынъ Ярославль, а самъ сѣдѣ на столѣ.[7]

This passage has caused some confusion amongst scholars. Both the 1915 editor of *N4* and D. S. Likhachev took the words *khorobri torovi* to be a corruption of *Khorobrita*, which, they claim, was the sobriquet of Mikhail Yaroslavich.[8] In other words the passage implies that after Svyatoslav's reign Andrey ousted his brother Mikhail. However, the only source to mention that Mikhail Yaroslavich was nicknamed

---

[5] *PSRL*, i, col. 472; Priselkov, op. cit. (n. 2), 323.

[6] For further speculation on the origins of *LN*, see Yu. A. Limonov, *Letopisanie Vladimiro-Suzdal'skoi Rusi* (L., 1967), ch. vii. Limonov considers that *LN* derived from a Rostov *svod* of 1278 (the year of the last dated item of *LN*), which itself had as one of its sources the 1276 redaction of the grand-princely chronicle (1276 is the year of the last Vladimir item in *LN*).

[7] *PSRL*, iv, chast' 1, vyp. 1 (Petrograd, 1915), 229. *Knyazhiv v Volodimere leto* is presumably an error for *knyazhiv . . . let 9*, cf. *LN: sede . . . Yaroslav . . . let 9*.

[8] *PSRL*, iv, 229; D. S. Likhachev, *Tekstologiya* (M.–L., 1962), 78. Note that both call him Mikhail *Aleksandrovich*.

Khorobrit is the sixteenth-century Nikon Chronicle (see below, n. 22);
and furthermore both the context (there is no mention of Mikhail
ousting Svyatoslav in the first place) and the word order (*Andrey* khorobri torovi *syn Yaroslavl'*) make it quite clear that according to *N4* it was
Svyatoslav who was driven out by Andrey, and not Mikhail. As for the
incomprehensible *khorobri torovi*, a possible clue is given by two other
manuscripts of *N4*: the hitherto unpublished 'Karamzin' manuscript
of *N4*, which in all probability represents the original redaction of *N4*,
has *Andrey Khorobritov*;[9] while in the Khronograf manuscript of *N4* (the
so-called Novgorod Fifth Chronicle)[10] we find . . . *Andrey Khorobritovich'*
(var. *Khorobritorovich'*) *syn Yaroslavl'*. These two additional sources might
well imply that Andrey's father Yaroslav was known as *Khorobrit*,
although there is no corroboratory evidence in other chronicles.

The similarity between the two versions, *N4* and *LN*, is too striking
to be fortuitous, and we can only assume that the compiler of *N4* was
influenced either by *LN* or by its source, the Rostov version of the grand-
princely chronicle of Vladimir. This, in fact, is borne out by other striking
similarities between the two chronicles: for example, *LN* and *N4* are
the only sources to mention a 'second census' which took place in 6781
(1273-4).[11] The existence of such similar items, which are not found in
the Sofiiskii First Chronicle (abbr. *S1*), would imply that they were
transmitted from *LN* to *N4* not via the '*svod* of 1448' (the hypothetical
common source of *N4* and *S1*), but either directly or via the Rostov
source of *LN*.

The only other chronicles in which there is mention of the forcible
removal of Svyatoslav by Andrey are the *Rogozhskii letopisets* (abbr. *R*)
and the Vladimir Chronicle (*Vladimirskii letopisets*) (abbr. *V*).[12] The first
of these, after recording items similar to those found in *L* and *T* under
6754 and 6755 (6754: death of Yaroslav; 6755: Svyatoslav's accession;
Aleksandr's and Andrey's journey to Mongolia), inserts under 6756 (one
year after Aleksandr and Andrey had set off to Mongolia!):

> Того же лѣта прогнанъ бысть великіи князь
> Святославъ Андреомъ княземъ Ярославичемъ.

[9] I am grateful to Professor Ya. S. Lur'e for this information. The 'Karamzin' manuscript
is in the Leningrad Public Library (F. IV. 603). For its relationship to the other manuscripts
of *N4*, see Ya. S. Lur'e, 'Obshcherusskii svod — protograf Sofiiskoi I i Novgorodskoi IV
letopisei', *Trudy Otdela drevnerusskoi literatury*, xxviii (1974). Cf. A. A. Shakhmatov, *Obozrenie
russkikh letopisnykh svodov XIV—XVI vv.* (M.-L., 1938), 189-95.

[10] *PSRL*, iv, chast' 2, vyp. 1 (Petrograd, 1917), 219.

[11] ...2-е число бысть от Адама 6781	В лѣто 6781... бысть число
лѣт(о) (*LN*)	2-е... (*N4*)

Cf. *s.a.* 6760 (1252-3): приде Неврюнь... и прогна и [= Андрѣя] за море (*LN*);
приде Неврюи... и прогна Андрѣя Ярославича за море (*N4*). There is also an
interesting similarity here with the Suzdal' Chronicle (*Moskovsko-Akademicheskii spisok*)
(*PSRL*, i, col. 524), which, in Limonov's opinion, derived from a source close to *LN*.

[12] *PSRL*, xv, col. 31; ibid. xxx (M., 1965), 91.

No mention is made of the return of Aleksandr and Andrey from Kara-korum, and nothing more is said about Andrey until 6759, when both his flight to Sweden after Nevryui's campaign and his death at the hands of the Chud' are briefly reported. Now Shakhmatov and Lur'e consider that the early part of *R*—up to 6796 (1288)—is a conflation of an unspecified thirteenth-century Suzdal' chronicle (i.e. a source close to *L* and *T*) and either the 'svod of 1448', or, more likely in Lur'e's opinion, a special redaction of *N4*.[13] In this particular instance the Rogozhskii account is little more than an unintelligent blending of a version close to that of *L* and *T* on the one hand (i.e. the Suzdal' chronicle source) and a version similar to that of *LN* and *N4* on the other. Whether in fact the compiler of *R* had at his disposal the Rostov source of *LN*[14] or *N4* itself cannot be stated for certain; but in view of the general similarities between *R* and *N4* for most of the thirteenth century it would seem more probable that *R* here derived from *N4*.

The compiler of *V*, who clearly had before him versions of the same two basic accounts,[15] made more intelligent use of them to provide a credible story. The chronology is identical to that of *L* and *T*:

> 6754: death of Yaroslav
> 6755: Svyatoslav accedes to the throne
> Aleksandr and Andrey set off to Mongolia
> 6757: Aleksandr and Andrey arrive back *ot Kanovich'*.

At this point the compiler of *V*, instead of the wording found in the Laurentian-Trinity account:

...и приказаша Олександрови Кыевъ... а Андрѣи сѣде в Володимери на столѣ

has:

князю Александру приказаша Киевъ... а князю Андрѣю дасть[?] Воло-димерь (cf. Nikon Chronicle. See below, n. 22),

to which he adds:

того же лета князь Андрѣи съгна дядю своего Святослава съ княжения из Володимеря и Суздаля, а сам сѣде в Володимери...

---

[13] A. A. Shakhmatov, *Obozrenie* (n. 9), 312–16; Ya. S. Lur'e, 'Troitskaya letopis'' (n. 1).

[14] Limonov considers that *R* used a source similar to that of *LN*. See Limonov, op. cit. (n. 6), 145–6.

[15] Little is known of the textual history of *V*. Tikhomirov believed it to be an abridgement of, or an extract from, a major sixteenth-century *svod*, close in its origins to *T* and some Novgorodian *svod*. See M. N. Tikhomirov, 'Letopisnye pamyatniki byvshego Sinodal'nogo (Patriarshego) sobraniya', *Istoricheskie zapiski*, xiii (1942), 257–62. A detailed examination of the years 1240–64 shows that it stemmed basically from the 'svod of 1448' (i.e. *N4* and *S1*) and from a *svod* close to that of 1408/9 (*L* and *T*). On three occasions it differs from both: 6753: eclipse (unique); 6755: Sartak's accession (only in *R*); 6757: removal of Svyatoslav by Andrey (only in *R* and *LN*).

L. L. Murav'eva considers that the compiler of *V* used a Novgorod source which was at the basis of *N4* (L. L. Murav'eva, 'Novgorodskie izvestiya Vladimirskogo letopistsa', *Arkheo-graficheskii ezhegodnik za 1966* (M., 1968), 37–40), a view shared by Lur'e (see Ya. S. Lur'e, 'Troitskaya letopis'' (n. 1)).

Thus the resulting version represents an intelligent attempt to blend two separate versions.[16]

The following stemma illustrates the above remarks: the symbols *L*, *T*, etc., refer to the versions found in the chronicles and not necessarily to the entire chronicles themselves; squares represent hypothetical *svody* or sources; broken lines indicate the possible intervention of other redactions:

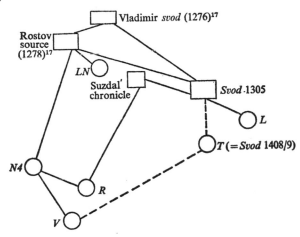

Now, if in fact Andrey ousted Svyatoslav, or if the version common to *LN* and *N4* (as well as *R* and *V*) reflects the original version of the story, then we can assume that this information was probably included in the Vladimir *svod* of 1276 (and certainly in the Rostov source of 1278), but that it was removed from the Vladimir grand-princely chronicle some time between 1276 and 1305. This removal probably took place at the time when the chronicle came under the influence of the principality of Tver' in the early fourteenth century; it must be remembered that Mikhail Yaroslavich, who became grand prince in 1304, was the son of Andrey's staunchest ally. The same information is given in the Tsarskii manuscript of *S1* (abbr. *S1(Ts)*),[18] except that here Mikhail is not called

---

[16] The attempts of the compiler of *V* to coalesce two different versions of the same event are not always so successful: see, for example, the description of Yaroslav Yaroslavich's fate after the battle of Pereyaslavl' (6760). According to one version originating in *L*, Yaroslav went from Tver' to Ladoga in 6762; according to the second, originating in the Novgorod First Chronicle, he fled to Pskov in 6761, and two years later was installed upon the throne of Novgorod. In the version found in *V* he flees to Pskov in 6761, and in the following year quits his patrimony (i.e. Tver') and goes to Ladoga! Cf. also s.a. 6749: *khodishya Nemtsy Novugorodu Velikomu Yavelyane [Vel'yadtsi?]*, which appears to be a contamination of the accounts found in *N4* and *S1* of the 'German' capture of Izborsk in 1240 (*Nemtsi, Medvezhane, Vel'yadtsi, Yur'evtsi*) and Aleksandr's capture of Kopor'e in 1241.

[17] Limonov's conjecture. See above, n. 6.

[18] *PSRL*, v (izd. 2-e), vyp. 1 (L., 1925), 236. According to this edition of *S1* the information is given in a gloss of the Synodal manuscript, while in the Tsarskii manuscript two similar entries, one under 6754 and one under 6756, are both crossed out.

Moskovskii. Very close to these three accounts is that found in the *Ustyuzhskii letopisnyi svod* (abbr. *U*):

В лѣто 6756. Князь великии Ярослав Всеволодовичь... преставися во Ордѣ нужною смертию.

В лѣто 6757. Сѣде на великом княжении Володимерском брат Ярославль Святослав Всеволодовичь и седѣ лѣто едино, и прогна его князь Михаило Ярославичь, а сам сѣде.

В лѣто 6758. Князи руские на Перотвѣ литву побили; тогда ж убиен бысть князь великии Михаило Ярославичь володимерскии.[19]

How did this version originate? Lur'e has convincingly shown that the four chronicles in question all derive from a hypothetical *svod* compiled in 1472 in the Kirillo-Belozerskii Monastery (abbr. *KB 1472*).[20] But what were the sources of this *svod*? Certainly the Nikanorovskii Chronicle of 1472 (*PSRL*, xxvii) and the *svod* of 1448 (i.e. *N4* and *S1*), as well as a Novgorodian source[21]—but not in this particular instance, for the Nikanorovskii Chronicle, *S1* and the Novgorod First Chronicle are either void or contain no information relevant to the events in question. In order to investigate possible sources of the events of 1246-9 as reflected in *KB 1472*, we must consider the various versions of Mikhail's death found in other chronicles, for the story of his usurpation is exclusive to *SS*, *S1(Ts)* and *U*.[22]

As we have seen, according to the four versions emanating from *KB 1472* the 'Russian princes' defeated the Lithuanians, and 'Grand Prince Mikhail Yaroslavich of Moscow (or Vladimir)' was killed on the Protva river. Now *L* and *T* have a different version. There is no mention of the river Protva; the Russians defeat the Lithuanians *after* Mikhail's death; their victory is at Zubtsov on the upper Volga; Mikhail is not styled *Moskovskii*, *Vladimirskii*, or *velikii knyaz'*. The second entry for 6756 merely states that Mikhail Yaroslavich was killed by 'the pagan Lithuanians'; this is followed by a brief description of his burial in Vladimir and a note on the defeat of the Lithuanians.[23] This version is

---

[19] *Ustyuzhskii letopisnyi svod (Arkhangelogorodskii letopisets)* (M.-L., 1950), 47.

[20] Ya. S. Lur'e, 'Istochnik "Sokrashchennykh letopisnykh svodov kontsa XV v." i Ustyuzhskogo letopistsa', *Arkheograficheskii ezhegodnik za 1971 god* (M., 1972), 120-9.

[21] I am grateful to Professor Lur'e for this information.

[22] Only the sixteenth-century Nikon Chronicle contains a composite version of what the compiler found in (a) *KB 1472* and (b) whatever version of the 'official account' (i.e. based on *L* and *T*) he had before him: after Yaroslav's death Svyatoslav ascends the throne (6755); in the following year: *knyaz' Mikhailo, naritsaemyi Khorobrit... sogna... Svyatoslava*, after which comes a version of the death of Mikhail ('Grand Prince of Vladimir') close to that of *L* and *T*. Finally in 6757 Aleksandr and Andrey return *ot konovich':... a ... Andreyu dasha* [cf. *dast'* in *V*] *velikoe knyazhenie v Volodimeri*. *PSRL*, x (M., 1965), 134, 136-7. The sobriquet *Khorobrit* may be a misunderstanding of *N4*'s account (*Andrey Khorobritovich'* in the Khronograf manuscript, see above, n. 10).

Tatishchev, drawing as usual from the Nikon Chronicle, has a thoroughly garbled version of the whole affair. See V. N. Tatishchev, *Istoriya Rossiiskaya*, v (M.-L., 1965), 39.

[23] *R* is almost identical, although the description of the burial is omitted.

repeated in the Moscow *svod* of 1479, although the victory over the Lithuanians is converted into an act of vengeance for Mikhail's death:

Князи *же* Суждальскые, братья Михаилова, идоша на Литву и биша их у Зубцева.[24]

Almost the same wording is found in the Ermolinskii and Nikon Chronicles, which would indicate that the version of *L* and *T* found its way into the so-called '*svod* of Metropolitans Feodosy and Filipp (1464–72)'.[25]

Only two chronicles, Part I of the *Tverskoi sbornik* (*TS(I)*) and *N4*, have accounts similar to that of *KB 1472*. We need not concern ourselves with the first of these: it is a late (1534) blend of both versions, i.e. that of *KB 1472* (Mikhail is called *Moskovskii* and the Protva is mentioned) and that of *L* and *T* (he is buried by Kirill, and his brother (singular) defeats the Lithuanians at Zubtsov).[26] *N4*, however, is strikingly similar to the versions of *SS*, *S1(Ts)*, and *U*:

В лѣто 6757... Тои же зимы... Князи Суздальстіи побиша Литву у Зубцева. А Михаилъ Ярославличь Московьскій убиенъ бысть от Литвы на Поротвѣ.

Now, this similarity could either mean that one of the sources of *N4* was *KB 1472*, or that *N4* and *KB1472* shared a common source. As there is no evidence elsewhere of readings common to *N4*, *SS*, *S1(Ts)*, *U*, and *TS(I)* but dissimilar to those of other chronicles, we must assume that the latter is the case. Thus the following stemma can be constructed:

[24] *PSRL*, xxv, 141.

[25] See Nasonov, op. cit. (n. 1), 268 ff. Note that the Ermolinskii Chronicle also derived from *KB 1472*, but mainly for the events of 1425–72. For pre-1425 events its main source was the *svod* of Feodosy and Filipp.

[26] *PSRL*, xv, col. 395. The description of Mikhail's burial and the defeat of the Lithuanians at Zubtsov is identical to that of the *svod* of 1518 (*PSRL*, xxviii (M.–L., 1963)), itself an indirect source of the protograph of the Ermolinskii Chronicle. For *TS(I)*'s dependence on this *svod*, see A. N. Nasonov, 'Letopisnye pamyatniki Tverskogo knyazhestva', *Izvestiya Akad. nauk SSSR, Otdel gumanitarnykh nauk* (1930), no. 9, pp. 709 ff.; for the sources of the *svod* of 1518, see Ya. S. Lur'e, 'Novye pamyatniki russkogo letopisaniya kontsa XV v.', *Istoriya SSSR*, 1964 no. 6, pp. 118–31; on *TS(I)*'s derivation from *KB 1472*, see Lur'e, 'Istochnik' (n. 20), 127–8.

It is clear that amongst the chronicle accounts of both halves of the story (the ousting of Svyatoslav and the death of Mikhail) $N4$ occupies a special position, differing as it does from the 'official' version as represented by L and T and their derivatives. There were two quite separate sources from which it derived:

1. The source of LN, R, and V, according to which Andrey usurped the throne of Vladimir and Mikhail was killed by the Lithuanians, who were then defeated by the Russians at Zubtsov.
2. The common source of SS, $S1(Ts)$, U, and $TS(I)$, according to which Mikhail of Moscow ousted his uncle and assumed the title of grand prince before being killed on the Protva river. From the first of these the compiler of the $N4$ version took the news of Andrey's usurpation of the throne and the name of the place at which the Russians defeated the Lithuanians (Zubtsov); from the second—Mikhail's appellation (*Moskovskii*) and the name of the river on which he was killed (*na Porotve*).

But why and how did the tale of Mikhail's usurpation of the throne of Vladimir arise in the first place? Before we can attempt to answer this we must consider the question of the likelihood of the story: was Mikhail prince of Moscow and did he ever become grand prince of Vladimir? These questions can be answered only *e silentio*. Firstly, no Muscovite source mentions Mikhail amongst the princes of Moscow,[27] nor is there any evidence to show that the town and district of Moscow was ever an *otchina* of anybody before it was given to Daniil Aleksandrovich in the second half of the thirteenth century. And secondly, no list of grand princes mentions Mikhail Yaroslavich.[28] From this negative evidence it seems most unlikely that Mikhail was prince of Moscow; indeed if he was, why should the fact have been so carefully concealed by the official chroniclers of Moscow? And it seems certain that he was never grand prince of Vladimir.

Why then did an unknown *svodchik* invent the story of 'Mikhail Moskovskii's' usurpation of the throne of Vladimir? A possible explanation may be that when in the early fourteenth century, at the time of the bitter rivalry between Tver' and Moscow, the grand-princely chronicler saw fit to remove from the records the original entry concerning Andrey Yaroslavich's usurpation, which in all probability took place, he invented and substituted the story of Mikhail; and in

---

[27] In the *Rodoslovets russkikh knyazei* appended to *SS* Mikhail is included under the sons of Yaroslav as *Mikhailo*, whereas Daniil is listed under the sons of Aleksandr Nevskii as *Danilo Moskovskii* (*PSRL*, xxvii, 298, 367). Cf. *Novgorodskaya pervaya letopis' starshego i mladshego izvodov* (M.–L., 1950), 466.

[28] For example, those preceding the Komissionnyi manuscript of the Novgorod First Chronicle. See ibid. 465 ff.

order still further to exacerbate Muscovite feelings he appended *Moskov-skii* to his name, thus providing a Moscow scapegoat for the arbitrary expulsion of Svyatoslav and the infringement of the law of succession by seniority. The emended version, however, did not last for long. It, too, was excised from the grand-princely chronicle, and we are left with the unsatisfactory and uninformative 'official' version which survived in the Laurentian and Trinity Chronicles.

Recent Publications Received[1]

GENERAL

New Zealand Slavonic Journal. No. 11. Wellington: Department of Russian, Victoria University, 1973. Pp. 164. 25 cm.

Bibliography

BIRKOS, A. S., and TAMBS, L. A., *Academic Writer's Guide to Periodicals*, II. *East European and Slavic Studies*. Kent, Ohio: Kent State University Press, 1973. Pp. 572. 23 cm. $10.00 ($7.50 paper).

EGEBERG, E., *Norsk litteratur om de slaviske og baltiske folks kultur, 1972: Materialer til en bibliografi* (Universitetet i Oslo, Slavisk-Baltisk Institutt, Meddeleser, 3). Oslo: Slavisk-Baltisk Institutt, 1973. Pp. 29. 21 cm.

Philology

GALLIS, A., *Beiträge zur Syntax der Richtungsverba in den slavischen Sprachen* (Skrifter utgitt av Det Norske Videnskaps-Akademi i Oslo, II Hist.-Filos. Klasse, Ny Serie 12). Oslo: Universitetsforlaget, 1973. Pp. 300. 27 cm. Nkr. 80.

MINISSI, N., *Unnützlichkeit der Phonemtheorie* (Euroasiatica: Folia philologica AION-Sl., Suppleta II: 2). Napoli: Istituto Universitario Orientale, 1973. Pp. 7. 24 cm.

ROT, A. M., *Vengersko-vostochnoslavyanskie yazykovye kontakty*. Budapest: Akadémiai Kiadó, 1973. Pp. 573. 24 cm. £9·20.

VALLE, M. V., *Rapporto tra l'evoluzione del sistema vocalico e l'"armonia" in protofinnico* (Euroasiatica: Folia philologica AION-Sl., Suppleta II: 1). Napoli: Istituto Universitario Orientale, 1973. Pp. 9. 24 cm.

BELORUSSIA

McMILLIN, A. B., *The Vocabulary of the Byelorussian Literary Language in the Nineteenth Century*. London: The Anglo-Byelorussian Society, 1973. Pp. 335. 29 cm. £2.

CZECHOSLOVAKIA

HOUGARD, C., *Tjekkoslovakiet i Danmarks spejl*. Odense: Universitetsforlag, 1971. Pp. 78. 21 cm.

Staročeský slovník, 4 (nedobře-neosědlý). Praha: Academia, 1972. Pp. 433–592. 24 cm.

POLAND

The Polish Review. Vol. xviii, no. 3. New York: The Polish Institute of Arts and Sciences in America, 1973. Pp. 128. 23 cm.

SCHENKER, A. M., *Beginning Polish*. Revised ed. 2 vols. New Haven and London: Yale University Press, 1973. Pp. xviii, 489; xi, 452; map. 25 cm. £4·25 (£2·95 paper) per vol.

YURIEFF, Z., *Joseph Wittlin* (Twayne's World Authors Series, 224). New York: Twayne Publishers, 1973. Pp. 175. 20 cm.

RUSSIA

BAER, J. T., *Vladimir Ivanovič Dal' as a Belletrist* (Slavistic Printings and Reprintings, 276). The Hague and Paris: Mouton, 1972. Pp. 204. 24 cm. 42 Gldrs.

BASILY, N. DE, *Diplomat of Imperial Russia, 1903–1917: Memoirs* (Hoover Institution Publications, 125). Stanford, Cal.: Hoover Institution Press, 1973. Pp. x, 201; 7 pls. 24 cm. $6.

---

[1] This list includes titles of volumes received since the publication of *OSP*, N.S., vol. vi. Authors and publishers can contribute to the usefulness of future lists by sending copies of their publications to the journal, c/o The Queen's College, Oxford, OX1 4AW.

BAZYLOW, L., *Społeczeństwo rosyjskie w pierwszej połowie XIX wieku*. Wrocław, etc.: Zakład Narodowy im. Ossolińskich, 1973. Pp. 507. 24 cm. Zł. 88.

BROWN, C., *Mandelstam*. Cambridge: University Press, 1973. Pp. viii, 320; 8 pls. 22 cm. $4·75.

Československá rusistika. xviii (3). Praha: Academia, 1973. Pp. 97–144. 23 cm.

FENNELL, J., ed., *Nineteenth-century Russian Literature: Studies of Ten Russian Writers*. London: Faber & Faber, 1973. Pp. 356. 22 cm. £6·50.

GARRARD, J. G., ed., *The Eighteenth Century in Russia*. Oxford: Clarendon Press, 1973. Pp. xiii, 356; 24 pls. 22 cm. £6·50.

KJETSAA, G., *Evgeny Baratynsky, zhizn' i tvorchestvo*. Oslo–Bergen–Tromsö: Universitetsforlaget, 1973. Pp. xiv, 739. 22 cm. Kr. 95.

—— *Leksika stikhotvorenii Lermontova. Opyt kolichestvennogo opisaniya* (Universitetet i Oslo, Slavisk-Baltisk Institutt, Meddelelser, 2). Oslo: Slavisk-Baltisk Institutt, 1973. 20 cm.

LAVRIN, J., *A Panorama of Russian Literature*. London: University of London Press, 1973. Pp. 325. 24 cm. £5.

MURAVIEV, P., *Vremya i den'*. New York: Continent Publishers, 1973. Pp. 334. 23 cm. $7.50.

PETERS, J.-U., *Turgenevs 'Zapiski ochotnika' innerhalb der očerk-Tradition der 40er Jahre* (Slavistische Veröffentlichungen, Ost-Europa Institut an der Freien Universität Berlin, 40). Wiesbaden: O. Harrassowitz, 1972. Pp. viii, 141. 24 cm.

PITCHER, H., *The Chekhov Play: a New Interpretation*. London: Chatto & Windus, 1973. Pp. viii, 224. 22 cm. £3.

YUGOSLAVIA

Čakavska rič. God 3, br. 1. Split: Matica hrvatska, 1973. Pp. 166. 24 cm.

POTTHOFF, W., *Die Dramen des Junije Palmotić: ein Beitrag zur Geschichte des Theaters in Dubrovnik im 17. Jahrhundert* (Bausteine zur Geschichte der Literatur bei den Slaven, Bd. 2). Wiesbaden: Franz Steiner Verlag, 1973. Pp. 360. 23 cm.

Slovo. Br. 22. Zagreb: Staroslavenski Institut 'Svetozar Ritig', 1972. Pp. 192; 4 pls. 24 cm.